The Hitch Hiker's Guide To Agile Coaching

by

The agile42 Coaches

The Agile Coaching Company

The Agile Coaching Company

agile42 International GmbH
Grünberger Str. 54, 10245 Berlin, Germany
Tel: +49 30 200 539 58
Web: www.agile42.com
Email: info@agile42.com

Edition: first edition, 2017-07-31

ISBN 978-3-96243-000-9 (printed, A5)
ISBN 978-3-96243-005-4 (printed, 5.5" x 8.5")
ISBN 978-3-96243-001-6 (ePub)
ISBN 978-3-96243-002-3 (Kindle)
ISBN 978-3-96243-003-0 (online PDF)
ISBN 978-3-96243-004-7 (promotional excerpt, 5.5" x 8.5")

Contents

Chapter 1

Introduction

Agile coaching is at heart not such a complicated thing. It is the art of observing, listening, forming an understanding and validating it, then working with the coachee to come up with and enact solutions. By coaching and observing others coach, you build up your own collection of patterns and tools. Where a junior coach will have to rely on written material and the support of others, an experienced coach can quickly form and validate hypotheses and pick the right tools from the toolbox.

But starting out as a new agile coach is not so easy. Where do you go? How do you get started? With this book we wanted to create an introductory reference for new agile coaches as well as experienced ScrumMasters. It contains much of the theory that we teach our new colleagues at agile42 and hopefully a lot of insights for new coaches. The intention was to provide a secondary source for what we teach as a lasting memory to hand out to clients and students. We decided to publish it so that even more people can enjoy the results.

What you are reading right now is the book we wish we had had when we started out as agile coaches.

Despite the title this book is not about *agility* as such. We will assume that the reader has a working knowledge of all things agile. We may touch on the agile principles and lean thinking in this book, but we are not going to explain e.g. why it makes sense to slice large work items into smaller independent pieces, or how to choose between synchronized and unsynchronized releases. There are plenty of good books around for those purposes.

We have tried to introduce the topics sequentially, so that later chapters build on top of previous ones. The book therefore wanders between different topics, although there is a clear path from listening to one-on-one coaching and onward to team coaching and how to empirically influence the behavior of a team. We do recommend that you at least skim the preceding chapters before jumping into later chapters.

Throughout the book we will use the term *agile coach*, but don't take that too literally. It's an umbrella term that covers everyone interested in coaching agile teams and small organizations. We don't expect that every reader wants to become an agile coach. Rather we have designed and written this book to be useful to a large number of people including ScrumMasters, development managers and system thinkers. So whenever you see "agile coach", please substitute it with whatever title you feel is appropriate for you.

That said, some parts of this book are written for people who see a lot of different teams, either inside one organization or across many companies. ScrumMasters, development managers and internal agile coaches typically work with the same teams year after year. Agile coaches, on the other hand, are expected to train and coach teams from scratch until they become self-sufficient in Scrum, which usually takes 2–3 months, before moving on to other teams. Over time a consulting agile coach will find herself working with many different teams in many different contexts and with many different goals. We have therefore included some material relevant to working with new teams. There are chapters and sections in this book dedicated to team building models, or what you can do to help your teams perform better.

At this point you may be wondering who these guys behind the book really are. We are agile coaches working at what we believe is the most awesome agile coaching company, agile42. Since this book was written by a team, we have chosen not to stand out individually. Instead, we have been writing this book as if it were software developed by a team.

This means that we started by formulating a strategic goal for why this book should be brought to life. We drew up a product vision from the user perspective; we named and described personas and created a story map. By planning tasks and visualizing them on a kanban board, we wrote the book through an iterative and incremental process. We focused on first developing a Minimal Viable Product (MVP) through a number of Minimal Marketable Features (MMF). What you see here is the MVP. For the software geeks among you, the book was entirely written using markdown files in a git repository with a continuous integration build using pandoc to create various formats of the book.

Becoming an agile coach is a journey that has no end. And that's why the name of this book is "The Hitchhiker's Guide to Agile Coaching."

Chapter 2

What is agile coaching?

Agile coaching is the art of helping people see reality using an agile and lean perspective and change their paradigms, habits and roles accordingly. Agile coaching has two very different sides — agility and coaching — and you will need to know a bit of both. Being good or skilled in only one of these two domains is not sufficient.

Agile is an umbrella term for all kinds of methods and practices that are based on the values and principles defined in the *Agile Manifesto* ("Agile Manifesto," 2001). At present the most widely used agile methods are Scrum, Kanban and XP. When we refer to "agile", we usually mean any and all of the agile methods, but we will sometimes specifically address one of the agile methods.

In our experience, most agile coaches typically have a background as ScrumMasters, project managers, general managers, process specialists or quality managers. Working with different teams, they have noticed that they can help the teams work better by introducing or strengthening the team's agile thinking. At some point, they may start calling themselves agile coaches, or they keep their ScrumMaster title. Through failures and successes, they have slowly learned how to approach and work with different teams. They have started out as new agile coaches with reasonably good agile knowledge, but do not know enough about coaching. If you belong to this group, this book is for you.

Agile thinking and agile practices are easier to learn than coaching skills. There are agile books, Scrum training, workshops, conferences, communities and a lot more available, however for many people the main problem is, in fact, the unlearning of old thinking patterns.

Coaching is also a skill that you can pick up and improve on, although perhaps not as easily as agile knowledge. This is because coaching is a way of acting, almost a personal habit, and habits are notoriously difficult to change.

In order to become a good coach you must learn to observe and listen, to keep your own biases in control, to not jump to premature conclusions and to communicate well. This naturally affects how you are aware of yourself, how you react to other people and how others perceive you. Many people are unwilling to even start this journey. For example, people who enjoy the feeling of power that comes from bossing people around, do not necessarily want to give it up.

Agile coaching is not magical handwaving. It is a soft but very very structured skill. We don't want to encourage the perception that an agile coach can just walk into an organization, talk to people, run some workshops, slap stickies on flipcharts and turn everyone super-agile. Instead, we see agile coaching as structured and long-term work that stretches over months, sometimes years.

The difference between a newly started agile coach and an expert coach is simply that the expert knows more structures by heart and remembers more tools; and has more experience to help her choose the right tool or structure for the job. Where an experienced coach can pick and choose from memory, new coaches may need to consult lists, books or mentors and are perhaps more likely to occasionally choose the wrong tool for the job. We hope that this book will give you the tools and structures you need to become an effective agile coach.

We would encourage you to think of coaching as an additional set of tools in your leadership toolbox. Coaching is something you can try out and adopt gradually, tool by tool and technique by technique; and it is very likely that you will find the skills and tools in this book useful in many different situations. For example, the skill of listening will be very convenient when interacting with customers and colleagues, as well as your mother-in-law.

2.1 Other kinds of coaching

In this chapter we would like to position agile coaching by comparing it to two other well-known coaching domains: **systemic coaching** and **sports coaching**.

If you haven't heard about systemic coaching before, you can think of it as the classical therapy or counseling approach. Imagine a patient sitting in a comfortable lounger and a calm, neutrally dressed counselor in a hardback chair with a notepad in her hand, asking "And how can I help you today?"

A systemic coach works *with* the system. The information, interpretations, goals and actions all come from the coachee and the systemic coach merely facilitates discovery through discussion. She asks neutral, open-ended questions related to keywords that pop up in the discussion. For example "Tell me more about your time there?" or "How did the others react to this piece of news?"

Agile coaching borrows a lot from systemic coaching. However, where the systemic coach is non-directing, the agile coach usually has an agenda of making the team more agile. Both systemic coaches and agile coaches usually have a sponsor and have been hired to achieve a goal. The difference is that systemic coaches try not to impose their own thoughts and ideas in the discussions. For an agile coach, part of the goal is to act as a role model, infusing the organization with agile thinking and practices.

Sports Coach	Agile Coach	Systemic Coach
Sets goals and targets for the team	Supports the team, provides benchmarks	Accepts any result

Sports Coach	Agile Coach	Systemic Coach
Defines the team	May discuss roles with manager	Accepts the team as it is
Lays off non-performing team members	Helps team members find ways to improve	Helps team members find ways to improve
Tells the team what to do in a given situation	Outside the selected method, helps the team understand the approach in a given situation	Helps the team explore scenarios and choose which one to pursue
Has a somewhat linear understanding of cause and effect	Uses lean and agile thinking to understand cause and effects	Has a circular understanding of cause and effect
Very transparent emotions	Moderate display of emotions	Aspires to be neutral

An agile coach also works in quite similar ways to a sports coach. Whereas professional athletes know a lot about their sports and their main tool (the human body), many professional software developers are lacking in theoretical knowledge as well as practical experience. The barriers of entry into software development are very low and many software developers never receive sufficient formal education in their craft. At the same time, the pressure to release new features means that best practices are forgotten and people collect the wrong kinds of experience.

Exacerbating the issue, everyone wants to portray themselves as experts in order to keep their jobs. The more senior developers who could perhaps act as mentors and role models are all overworked, participating in dozens of critical projects and workgroups simultaneously. This means that agile coaches need to tread carefully when nurturing both basic software practices, as well as agile project/product management and team building practices.

Every coach should always have a *clear goal.* Unfortunately, agile coaches are often called in to do something vague or implicit, such as “we’ve been told to deploy Scrum” or “my team isn’t meeting their sprint goals” or “could you just look at this team and say what’s wrong?” Part of your job is therefore to observe or quickly assess the organization, make a diagnosis or draw up some hypotheses and agree on the goal with your sponsor. Without an understanding of what the organization wants and needs, it is difficult to achieve results.

To do this, you will need to allocate “access time” with the organization. In some cases, this might mean a concerted, structured assessment carried out in a very short time. Other times, it may be more informal and unstructured — to the extreme point of hanging around in the coffee room trying to meet and interview as many different people as possible.

2.2 The agile coaching stances

Interestingly enough, an agile coach needs to be able to do many different things that are *not* coaching. One of the basic skills of agile coaching is to understand when to coach and when not to coach and to know what else you might do instead.

For example, you may notice that a team doesn’t understand why they should split work into small independent tasks. If you were only allowed to coach, you would need to ask the right questions in sequence, patiently guiding them forward step by step until they connect the dots, understand the implications and come up with the right methods. This would require almost inhuman leaps of logic and induction from the team, as well as almost inhuman coaching skills from you. It would be more effective to just step out of the coaching role and spend a little moment as a teacher.

Coaching and teaching are two different "modes of operation" that we call *coaching stances*. There are five stances in total (see fig. 2.1) and we will explore them in this section. You should always be aware of which coaching stance you are taking at any given moment. You will change stances regularly as the situation dictates and you will need to take a different approach in each stance.

Coaching — For the most part, you should operate as a coach and stay in the base stance of coaching. This is where you listen and observe how the team works; challenge and question their assumptions and status quo; and facilitate and lead the activities.

The coaching stance is very close to systemic coaching as we described in the beginning of this chapter (in sec. 2.1). It is the most "neutral", in that the coach tries to be unbiased and not push her own ideas on the team. In order to avoid biasing the team that you are coaching, you should try to step back into the coaching stance as soon as the situation allows.

Teaching — The teaching stance that we mentioned in the beginning of this section is one that you will find yourself using quite a lot. In contrast to systemic coaches and to some extent also sports coaches, agile coaches need to be able to educate and teach people.

In this context, "teaching" means the ability to detect when the group you are coaching is lacking knowledge on some topic, explain the concepts in a clear way, answer questions related to those concepts, and verify that the group has indeed acquired the new knowledge. It does not necessarily mean planning and carrying out engaging, informative

Figure 2.1: The coaching stances

multi-day courses. Although many agile coaches also work as agile trainers and vice versa, the skillset required for giving multi-day courses is quite different.

As mentioned, you should find your way back from the teaching stance to the coaching stance as soon as possible. Asking questions like "How do you think this new knowledge will affect your future actions?" or "With the knowledge I just provided you, what will in your perspective be the best thing to do now?" can help you return to coaching. It also signals to the coachee that you are giving the responsibility back to her and she needs to make wise decisions with the new knowledge in mind.

Mentoring — This is the process of transferring learnings from the mentor to the mentored person, the *mentee*. The mentoring stance is useful when the mentee has knowledge to some extent, but lacks experience in the topic. The transfer of experience often happens through discussions, stories, anecdotes and advice. It can also happen through hands-on demonstrations or through collaboration and pair work, in which case one could talk about *apprenticeship*.[1]

Mentoring is often confused with coaching, possibly because a good mentor must also be a good listener and a good coach. Many mentoring programs contain aspects of career or life coaching. Similarly, coaches must sometimes act as mentors. An agile coach would most commonly mentor a junior agile coach or a ScrumMaster.

Your mentee is likely to find it convenient to have a mentor and she will encourage you to stay in that stance. Again, remember to return to the coaching role as soon as possible. For that, you can state something like "That was the story I wanted to tell you. What kind of thoughts did it give you?" or "Now that we have done this together, let me see you do it on your own."

"I refuse to answer that question on the grounds that I don't know the answer."
— Douglas Adams

Advising — Being an agile coach also includes the capability of giving advice to a client when necessary. This includes giving options, creating insights and evaluating their experiences. If you have opinions on a topic, you will also need to justify and motivate.

You should be very careful when giving advice, as coaching and advising are conflicting activities. As a coach you are

[1] See http://en.wikipedia.org/wiki/Mentorship and http://en.wikipedia.org/wiki/Apprenticeship

supposed to be neutral and unbiased, but as an adviser you are expected to provide opinions and suggestions. You cannot do both at once. This is one of the reasons why you are most likely better off adopting one of the other stances rather than advising.

Another reason is that people who ask for advice are not always looking for an honest answer. It happens that people just want to vent their frustration or would like to know whether they can use you for support when driving their own agenda.

The third reason is that when you give advice or recommendations, you must also take responsibility for that advice. Sometimes you should not have any say in the matter or you may have conflicting interests. Sometimes a simple question requires a complex answer (or several complex answers) and sometimes the client takes your answer and implements it without understanding the implications.

We commonly find ourselves answering “it depends” and then perhaps explaining the relevant theory (training), helping them find their own answer (coaching) or providing examples that are hopefully illuminating (mentoring). Only occasionally do we actually give straight-out answers (advising) and it almost never happens that we carry out the work for them (consulting).

Even when giving advice, you should always leave the responsibility to the coachee. One trick to make that happen is to form your suggestions as hypotheses: “Could it be a possibility for you to…?”, or provide several options: “Another approach that could be worth exploring is …” This sends a signal to the coachee that it is her call to come up with the solution, since she is the one that knows the context best. It also indicates that you are now stepping back to the coaching stance. When you push your solution onto someone else, there is a risk that the other person will not be fully committed to achieve the wanted result.

Role modeling — As agile coaches we constantly need to demonstrate integrity. Some of the key pillars in your career as an agile coach are transparency, honesty, commitment to help people grow and maximizing the benefits for your clients. Role modeling is primarily about living the agile and lean values.

An agile coach cannot simply say one thing and then do something else. For example, stating that meetings always start on time and then arriving late yourself, or asking the ScrumMaster to be prepared but showing up unprepared for your own engagements.

Role modeling is different from *contracting* or *consulting*. A contractor or consultant is hired to do a job on behalf of the client. The difference is that role modeling is a form of on-the-job training for the organization's own ScrumMasters. The role model also only assumes responsibility on a limited level and for a limited time e.g. ensuring that a retrospective is well facilitated or that the team is paying attention to the resulting actions.

As a role model you could for example facilitate a couple of sprints, gradually handing over to the organization's own ScrumMasters which falls nicely within the scope of almost any coaching engagement. This is in sharp contrast to sports coaches who typically do not go out on the field to score goals during a match, and to systemic coaches who can't change themselves on behalf of their clients.

If your coaching engagement explicitly includes contracting or consulting, we would talk about *embedded coaching*. An embedded agile coach is expected to work full time as a team member or ScrumMaster for a period of months or years and simultaneously roll out agile practices or promote agile thinking in the team and surrounding organization. While this may seem like a great idea — two for the price of one, so to speak — we try to avoid this mode of engagement as it has several pitfalls for both the coach and the client organization.

As the coach is now inside the organization, some of her credibility and leverage will be lost within months and managers will start bossing her around. Much of the coaching effort is spent on running the mechanics of the chosen agile method and the coaching progress is slower than it could be. The organization also easily becomes dependent on the coach, so that progress stagnates after the coach eventually leaves the building.

Embedded coaching is also problematic for the coach herself. Working with two different goals seldom leads to satisfactory results, especially if the goals are conflicting. There is only so much time… should I run a retrospective or write more software? Furthermore, personal professional development can come to a standstill. Compared to a dedicated agile coach, an embedded coach has twice the number of professions to learn about but even less time. The experience she collects will be limited to this particular client and she will lose out on the wide, generalized knowledge that comes from working with many diverse clients.

As an embedded coach, it is important to make it explicit when you are stepping from one role to another. Do not move constantly back and forth or linger in between, because that will only confuse people around you. You will also need to find somebody to train as your replacement.

As an agile coach you should always be careful not to involve yourself in content and product decisions when advising and role modeling. It may be tempting to propose new and nifty features or nudge the user interface just so. Remember that you have been engaged to improve the organization and not the product.

When you position yourself inside the system you are making it difficult to stay objective and unbiased. And unless you happen to be a recognized domain expert, it is very likely that the organization you are coaching understands their customers better than you do.

2.3 When not to coach

"It can be very dangerous to see things from somebody else's point of view without the proper training."
— Douglas Adams

Coaching requires a certain objectivity and it is difficult to coach people you deeply care for. Avoid coaching your family, friends or close business partners unless they really ask for it. Even then you might want to make clear that it's a one-off thing. Get out of your home or office, go to a coffee shop or take a walk while you discuss. And when the coaching session ends, remember to step out of the coaching mode and be yourself.

Sometimes you will meet individuals who mistake coaching for therapy or are messed up beyond the help of a coach. Coaching is not therapy. In these cases, we recommend that you gently back off and stay in coaching territory. This is primarily because amateur therapists can do serious damage, but also giving therapy is probably not what you were engaged for.

Now, of course, there are agile coaches who are also trained and licensed therapists. There might be situations where somebody engages such a trained and licensed therapist in order to give therapy to individuals or teams. If this is the situation, we are quite sure that you know it and can handle it. In all other cases, we recommend that you step back and let professionals with the right skills handle the issue.

How do you recognize that you are coaching a person who needs therapy more than coaching? The best advice we have heard is from a pilot in the context of landing an airplane: *If you are in doubt, then you are not in doubt!* Meaning that if you suspect that you are on the wrong path, then act as if you are on the wrong path.

2.4 Try this

1) When working with a team, regularly remind yourself of your coaching stance. Try to return to the base stance, coaching, as soon as possible.

2) The next time someone is asking for your advice, try a different stance than straight out advising. *Teach* the relevant underlying theory (in a nutshell). *Coach* them to bring out the pros and cons of different options. *Mentor* them by giving examples from other teams or organizations you have worked with.

Chapter 3

Coaching Fundamentals

"Attention is the currency of leadership."
— Ronald Heifetz

In sec. 2.1, we discussed how agile coaching compares to and contrasts with systemic coaching. In this chapter we will look more into the fundamentals of using systemic coaching approaches in your job as an agile coach.

We will focus on how to coach individuals as a systemic coach. Coaching teams is much easier once you know how to coach individuals. You do not need to be an expert personal coach though — even a little knowledge of personal coaching can help you a long way when coaching teams. We will cover techniques for listening and formulating questions and talk about how to structure discussions.

3.1 Code of conduct for a systemic coach

Let us first have a look at what a coaching relationship is. A coaching relationship is primarily a *powerless environment* (Stelter et al., 2005). This means the coachee and the coach are to be equal partners in the conversations. You coach eye to eye — not from above and not from below. The coachee should not have to be concerned about consequences for her job or career from what thoughts and ideas she is sharing with the coach. If she has, she will be holding back which will decrease the effect of the coaching.

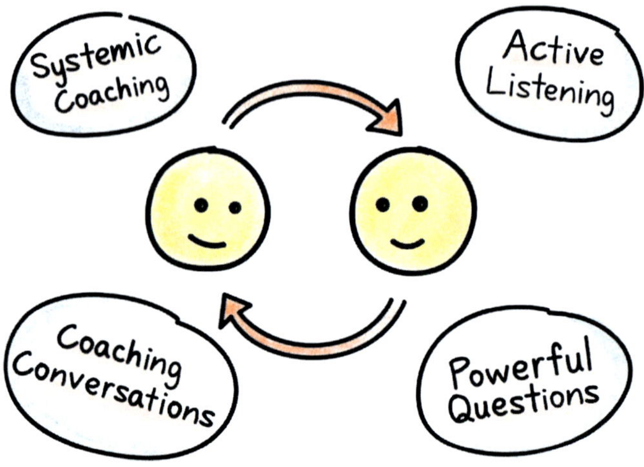

Figure 3.1: The fundamentals of coaching

Secondly, a coaching relationship is a *room with confidentiality*. The coachee should feel safe at all points in time, both during and after the conversation. This means that you do not share details from the conversation with others — at least, not without permission from the coachee. In popular terms, one could say that the *The Vegas Rule* applies here: What happens in the conversation, stays in the conversation. We will return to the topic of confidentiality when we talk about establishing a coaching conversation in sec. 3.5.

Finally, *it is over when it is over*. Meaning, you do not restart a coaching conversation once you have completed it. There is a time and place for the conversation. Within that you discuss challenges, you explore possibilities, you define action plans and you agree on how and when to follow up. Outside that the conversation is not going on. You do not refer or add on to the conversation when meeting the coachee at the coffee machine, in the canteen or anywhere else.

A coaching relationship can only exist within these restrictions. Always keep them in mind and, when necessary, make them explicit to the persons you are coaching.

3.2 The mindset behind systemic coaching

A coaching conversation is something that is co-created between the coachee and the coach. It is like a *dance* to which both parties contribute. In order to perform well, you must first agree about the purpose, the style, the rhythm and so on. If in a real dancing situation one tries to do a jitterbug while the other attempts a waltz, the mix-up will become apparent within the first few steps. In a coaching situation however, misunderstandings of similar magnitude can go undetected for a long time.

As coaching is an approach to help people grow, a positive mindset is also required. People grow through appreciation, by being acknowledged and respected for who they are, but also by being challenged by new and more ambitious goals. Appreciation is not about praising people for any random reason, but taking an approach like appreciative inquiry (Cooperrider and Whitney, 2005) as a starting point.

Appreciative inquiry is a research-backed approach where people in an organization collectively imagine and describe a compelling future. Because this future state is desirable, people don't have to be forced or incentivized into working their way there. Focusing on problems and how to solve them is wearying in the long run and might even make the problems bigger. You will find that several of the models we present in this book, e.g. the 5D model in sec. 4.2, follow the appreciative inquiry approach.

A catalyst for this is to live out the *Principle of Heliotropism*, which states that positive imagination leads to positive actions and results. By having positive ideas about the future we are already laying the foundation for this positive future. Positive thoughts create similar connections in our brains as if we already were acting according to these ideas. This frees up energy to see new possibilities and do constructive work towards achieving our goal. Like a sunflower we are orienting ourselves towards the sun and take advantage of the possibilities we are being given. One of the most well-known uses of the Principle of Heliotropism was President Obama's victory speech in Chicago Grant Park, November 4th 2008. His primary messages were *All things are possible*, *Changes are coming* and *Yes we can!*

With this in mind, let us dig into what tools and techniques you can use for successful coaching.

3.3 Curiosity and keywords

At the risk of stating the obvious, we would like to underline that a coach should be **curious and interested** in people. This is a self-selective trait: if you are not interested in people, you will find it very boring to work as an agile coach. So don't be afraid of asking questions. The only thing worse than being clueless about something is trying to hide that you are clueless. And frankly, who is the subject matter expert here — you or the coachee?

That said, if you keep asking random questions or repeat the same prepared questions, it sends a signal that you are not taking the conversation seriously. Make notes, review them and learn. People know that names and in-house acronyms are difficult to remember, so those are more excusable. And sometimes new tools or an organizational restructuring may cause what you have learned to become obsolete. Even so, the professional approach is to remember as much as possible or at least give the impression that you care.

Keywords are words that unlock further ideas and concepts. They depend almost totally on the coachee and the conversation and are not always easy to identify. We recommend that you keep notes, jotting down what you think could be significant. If some word pops up or is mentioned repeatedly, ask about it or underline the words so that you can return to them later. When there is a lull in the conversation, scan back and look for interesting and relevant topics to return to. "You mentioned … earlier. What does that mean?"

Asking about something may uncover more keywords. Jot them down too and use the new keywords in combination with your agile expertise to design more questions. There is a root cause analysis technique called "five whys," hinting at the fact that digging down five layers is usually enough. Sometimes there could be three layers and sometimes six, but on average the causal branch you are exploring will bottom out after five times of asking "and why does *that* happen?"

Be aware that it's entirely possible to dig too far. You should look out for circular answers and indications that the coachees are getting bored or fidgety. In a coaching conversation, you need to walk a fine line between going too wide and going too deep.

As a practicing agile coach you will stumble across patterns that repeat inside and across companies. Don't make the mistake of assuming that these similar patterns have similar solutions. Keywords most often point to symptoms, but the underlying network of causes and effects can be very complicated and not all of the causes are necessarily visible.

For example, many new Scrum teams (and sadly many established teams too) are struggling to meet their sprint goals. Clearly something does not work as it should… but what? Perhaps the Product Owner is pushy, perhaps the managers don't understand capacity planning, perhaps they are dependent on another team delivering an unreliable, low quality component? Perhaps all of the above… or something else? Don't make assumptions — go and see.

We will discuss this topic further in the chapter on structured coaching (sec. 7). For now, remember to be curious and keep track of keywords.

3.4 Listening and responding

We all think while we listen. We study the person whom we are in a conversation with, reflect on the words, tie back into our own experiences, find sudden insights or interesting parables and connections. Often our thoughts take us far away into our own spheres of interest and when we come back to reality we realize that we have missed something… but probably nothing important, right? Other times we find something really important to say and mull over the message, rehashing it in our own minds while we wait for our turn to speak… and forget to listen. This is how our brains are built and there is nothing wrong with that.

As coaches, however, these habits make it difficult for us to do our job. They take focus away from the coachee, and while we sometimes get good ideas, just as often we might jump to premature conclusions. As coaches, we need to listen better. In this section, we will cover some thinking models and effective techniques for listening.

Shifting or supporting

The *waiting-to-speak syndrome* occurs when the listener is not actually focusing on what the speaker is saying, but rather is waiting for a break in the flow in order to infuse her own thoughts into the discussion. When somebody does this to you it feels like the other person is not actually listening to what you said. In response, people often resort to repeating their words in a louder voice, rehashing their arguments in different words or speaking on top of the other person.

This syndrome is the result of what we call **shift response** — when we think more about how to shift the topic into whatever suits our purposes than about what the other person is saying. The opposite, **support response**, is when we are following along with the discussion in order to keep it flowing. In general there is nothing wrong with either kind of response and a good discussion needs a suitable combination of both.

When we are coaching, however, we need to be careful not to *drive* the discussion. We need to be aware of which response we are using. Support response is generally the gentler and safer option. We already mentioned keywords in sec. 3.3 as a way to stay focused and in sec. 3.6 we will discuss an effective method for creating questions that bring the conversation forward without disrupting the topic.

Communication enablers

Every serious traveller has experienced situations in which they need to communicate with someone but don't know the language. It can be something as simple as buying a meal or getting a taxi or something as complex as trying to explain what you do for a living — presumably some form of ScrumMastering or agile coaching. How do you explain agility if you only have five words in common? How about coaching?

Without a common language communication becomes slow and error-prone and is limited to simple and concrete things. If you can not point to it or show a picture of it, it does not exist. Having sufficient command of a *common language* is one of the basic communication enablers. As the name suggests, the enablers help the flow of communication. If you are missing one or more enablers, communication — and thereby also coaching — becomes difficult. If many or all enablers are missing, communication becomes impossible.

A *common culture* is another enabler, similar to a common language. People from different cultures look at the world differently and this can cause misunderstandings during discussions. Cultural differences can also cause *prejudices* which tend to prevent people from entering a conversation with open minds.

Listener *biases* and *emotions* likewise make it difficult to communicate. As an agile coach, you will often meet people who are just doing things wrong and refuse to understand it — in fact they may even try to convince you that your own methods will never work here. It may help to recognize that you are both biased in your own ways. Similarly, if a person is upset or sad, she may find it difficult to focus on the discussion. It could be a quarrel at home, some personal issues, perhaps bad news, sometimes just too little sleep or a headache.

For communication to be effective you will also need *enough time* and a *distraction-free environment.* For example, one of the authors of this book gets caught by moving images and finds it difficult to hold a discussion if a television is on in the background. Even an information radiator or a street window can be distracting. He solves this by picking seats that face away from the TV or window.

Furthermore, the communication channel should be as wide as possible.[1] Morse code or radio transmissions are at one extreme: these transmissions are very slow, unidirectional and require additional encoding and decoding. Videoconferencing tools are somewhere in the middle, although they have become much better over the last decade or so. Live face-to-face discussion is at the other extreme. In a live conversation, verbal communication is enhanced

[1] "The most efficient and effective method of conveying information… is face-to-face conversation." ("Agile Manifesto," 2001)

by postures, gestures, facial expressions and body movements. Information flows in both directions between the participants.

Active listening

Virginia Satir (1964) was the first to recognize that listening consists of several stages. She divides reception into intake, meaning, significance and response. As coaches, we like to use the simpler but still adequate **active listening model**[2] which contains the three phases of comprehending, retaining and responding.

In active listening, the first phase is *comprehending*. This includes hearing and understanding the words, sentences and the context. As mentioned above, understanding the language and the cultural context is very important and even critical for comprehension.

The second phase is *retaining*. The problem here is that speech is real-time, wide-band communication. The words come at you fast and it is not always possible to stop and consider a sentence from different perspectives or even ask the speaker to repeat. Other problems include the fact that short-term memory is lossy — previous sentences will be drowned out by new ones.

Further, it sometimes happens that you underestimate the significance of something when you first hear it. Later you get more information and realize that the speaker made some important point previously, but you can no longer remember exactly what it was. It is also easy to lose attention, especially in one-way presentations or in other situations where you are not expected to contribute.

The third phase is *responding*, which includes both verbal and nonverbal responses. Body language — a simple thing like raising a finger — can be a powerful way of reacting without actually breaking the flow of the speaker. Verbal responses come on different levels: we can repeat what we just heard word by word, we can paraphrase the message or we can add our own reflections to it. We might also

[2] http://en.wikipedia.org/wiki/Active_listening

bring the topic forward by replying in support or in contradiction, or perhaps shift the topic to something else.

The good news is that listening and responding is a skill at which you can become better. Let's focus on a model that may help you understand how listening works.

The levels of listening

There are different ways of listening, some of which are more suitable and some less suitable for coaching. Kimsey-House et al. (2011) describes three levels of listening that approximately map to first person (me), second person (you) and third person view (us). Let's describe these listening levels (see also fig. 3.2) and reflect on how they can be useful for an agile coach.

Figure 3.2: The levels of listening

Level 1 – Internal listening (subjective) — In level 1 listening, the narrator's story is reflected through the listener's own experiences and memories. Keywords remind you of episodes or topics that are of interest to you, but not necessarily to the speaker. It can trigger a premature reply, an unexpected shift response that cuts the flow and steers the discussion off topic.

For example, when hearing about somebody's misfortunes on the way to work, the listener may be prompted to tell about her own commute. Or when hearing somebody complain about a problem, the listener may feel obliged to solve it. Or when the speaker mentions a theory or method, the listener may be led to give a lecture on the topic complete with "interesting" examples.

Sometimes people just feel the need to vent and do not want much more than "tea and sympathy", compassion and support. Other times, they might be hoping for concrete advice related to some issue and might not be interested in hearing tangential stories. The speaker may be halfway through a story when she is interrupted and not allowed to finish. In all of these cases, the shift response may be quite rude to the original speaker. People may get the perception that the responder is selfish, trying to hijack the discussion or one-upping in an attempt to impress.

Of course, level 1 listening can also inject new and interesting information into a discussion. When mentoring, it can be useful to share personal experiences. A drink and a funny anecdote told at a party may trigger more drinks and even funnier anecdotes. In coaching conversations, however, level 1 is mostly out of place and should be used with care.

Level 2 – Focused listening (passive) — In level 2 listening, the listener is fully focused on sucking in information and committing it to memory. The story is heard without filters and the listener is almost sitting in the narrator's chair.

This can be a very effective way of learning about the other person. We use the VIBE model to remember what to observe when listening:

- Voice — the intonation, energy level, sighs and grunts
- Information — verbal (choice of words, what is said, what is left unsaid) and non-verbal (shrugging, pointing)
- Body language — hand gestures, changes in posture, facial expressions etc.
- Emotions — is the person coming across as happy, sad, distressed, calm, energetic, passive, neutral etc.

The main drawback of level 2 listening is that you sometimes forget to participate enough in the discussion and this can make the speaker nervous or distraught. This is because people subconsciously search for feedback while speaking. If the feedback is missing or contradictory, the speaker gets confused and doesn't know how to continue. Most people just sputter to a stop, thinking that the listener is trying to be mean or sarcastic. As a coach, this is not the message you want to send.

Level 3 – Global listening — Listening with empathy. Everything is included in the listening: the speaker's tone of voice, body language, changes in energy level, etc. The listener is not only listening to the voice and words of the speaker but also actively follows the non-verbal cues. Global listening requires patience and curiosity and the ability to put yourself in the shoes of the speaker.

Humans are social animals and we have evolved to use body language and facial expressions as well as prosody — the tone of voice, syllable stress and rhythm — when we communicate. Non-verbal cues give additional information that can be very useful in a coaching conversation. Often the cues support the verbal message, but sometimes they can seem irrelevant or even conflicting. Conflict in words and body language could for example indicate that the other person is stressed or distracted.

Other times you can pick up non-verbal information that changes or even inverts the meaning of the words. Sarcasm, for example, relies on tuning the verbal message just right. While people can express sarcasm just by choosing the appropriate (or inappropriate) words, it is much easier if they can use non-verbal channels as well.

Non-verbal communication is often more honest than verbal communication. That is, somebody might say one thing yet make it apparent from their stance and the tone they use that they would rather say something else. There are also microexpressions, visible emotions like disgust, anger and fear that flicker over the face for a fraction of a second. While they are difficult to catch, they are also almost impossible to suppress. People who know what to look for might gain a lot of information, such as whether the other person is being truthful or not.

That said, in the context of agile coaching, we are more interested in setting up a safe and constructive environment than constantly assessing the honesty of the coachee. Body language is too large and fuzzy a topic to fit in here, so we will not go into detail. Our message to you is to watch for gestures, postures, emotions, inflections, pauses etc., that indicate whether the coachee is alert and interested in the conversation. Combine this information with the spoken words to gain a more complete understanding of what is going on.

In addition to the three levels of listening, there are also several ways of *not listening*. One might ignore the other person completely or half-listen while doing other things. Obviously these are not good approaches for an agile coach. If you find yourself distracted to the point of listening with a half ear only or briefly ignoring the other person, the best thing you can do is apologize and either break the discussion or continue with renewed focus.

There is nothing particularly good or bad in any of the three levels. In fact, in a normal social conversation all three levels are needed in suitable amounts. In coaching conversations, however, level 1 and to some extent also level 2 can disturb the balance of the discussion and undermine the trust between coachee and coach. This is why an agile coach should continuously be aware of which level she is listening at and try to move towards levels 2 and 3.

Try this

1) You can try out the different levels of listening on a test subject in a short exercise of less than ten minutes. Explain the three levels, then ask the other person to tell you a story e.g. about what they did last weekend in three minutes. While they tell the story you will switch several times between the three levels of listening. After the story is finished, the storyteller should try to guess the sequence of listening levels that you used. You can also swap roles and run the exercise again.

2) If you notice that you are falling into level 1 listening, feeling a strong urge to tell of similar events or give solutions, you can try some of the following "survival techniques":

    - Focus on identifying and writing down keywords as you hear them, so that you can get them off your mind and onto paper where you can pick them up later. If the same keywords are repeated, underline them or draw boxes around them.
    - If you run out of keywords, also note your own ideas and hypotheses. One technique is to draw a vertical line

across the paper and write keywords and observations on the left and your own thoughts and hypotheses on the right.

- Ask neutral clarifying questions related to the keywords you pick up: "Tell me more about ...", "What do you mean when you say ...?", "What was the impact of ...?" or "Why do you think they acted that way ...?" Don't try to help the other person or create any development in the discussion.
- In your own mind, quickly and silently repeat the words the other person is saying. This technique is known as "rapid repeating" and it helps with clearing out your own thoughts.
- Don't talk, use only non-verbal signals (sounds, expressions, grunts and body language) to keep the conversation going.
- Limit yourself to replies of one or two syllables ("Yes", "OK", "Mhm?", "And then?" ...) to keep the conversation going without injecting topics.
- Admit that you got lost in the discussion: "Sorry, I was distracted/had to write something down. Could you repeat what you just said?"
- Repeat back what you heard to confirm your understanding (active listening). You can repeat exactly what you heard word by word (verbatim) or describe it in your own words (paraphrasing).
- Adjust your own posture to change the dynamics. Lean forward or back, cross/uncross your legs or just relax in the chair. When the topic changes, you can take it as a cue to change your posture.
- Mirror the other person's body posture and voice level. This technique is known as "pacing".
- Apply some "mindfulness" in your listening. Without removing your focus from the speaker, try to relax and make your awareness wider. Open up your senses to

take in as much of the environment you can.

3) The next time you are in a place with many others — a lounge, classroom, concert, shopping mall, beach, park, restaurant, football match, train station etc. — take a moment to apply level 3 listening on the whole room. Observe what is happening. What groups can you see? Who is talking to whom? Are people energetic, expectant, stressed, happy or sad?

3.5 Structure for a coaching conversation

A coaching conversation is not just small talk about how things are going or not going. Coaching conversations are for committed individuals or teams that want to make a significant change or get wiser about an important matter. To help you succeed as a coach, you can apply a structure to the coaching conversation. This helps you and the coachee (or team) to focus on the important topics and find specific actions to carry out as results of the conversation.

It is important to remember that a coaching conversation is something that you design together with the persons you are working with, at the moment when the conversation is wanted. As a coach you never take the coachee or team to places they do not want to go — this would be strictly out of line. You should never guide the content of the discussion, nor force somebody into a discussion. What you do instead is help them to go where they want to go, while helping them reflect on what is important.

As the coach, your task is to make sure that the environment is right. In sec. 3.4, we mentioned the important communication enablers. Try to ensure that all of them are in place. Allocating enough time and setting up a distraction-free environment is easy, but if there are large cultural differences or you lack a common language you may have to reconsider whether the conversation is worth having at all.

We have found that many people do not know what coaching looks like. Sometimes they just need to vent or want some advice and get upset when you start by asking questions. In such situations, we have found it useful to ask for permission to coach, for example, by saying: *"Is it ok if I ask you some questions to help you achieve the result you want to achieve?"*

The two levels of the coaching conversation

As shown below in fig. 3.3, a coaching conversation is conducted on two levels: A) the conversation level and B) the meta level (Storch et al., 2006). As the coach you are constantly acting on both levels. The coachee or team is primarily on the conversation level, but will from time to time be invited to the meta level by you.

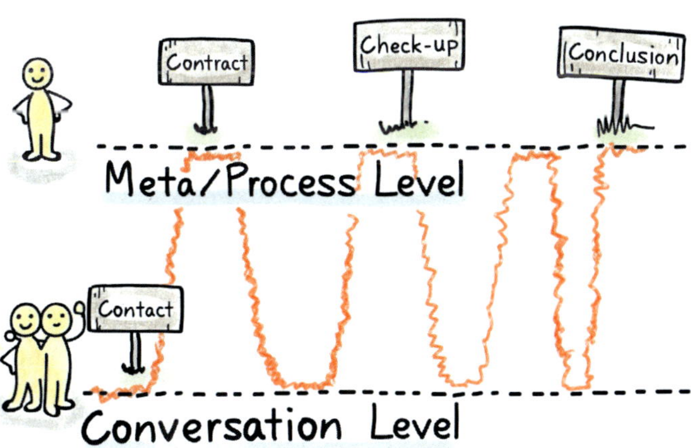

Figure 3.3: The structure of a coaching conversation

The *conversation level* is where the actual conversation happens. Here you are using the levels of listening, showing curiosity and forming questions based on keywords as we discussed previously. The coachee or team are also on this level as they answer your questions.

The *meta level* is where you are observing, reflecting and designing the conversation. Here you are deciding which powerful questions[3] to ask, which hypotheses to formulate and in which direction to take the conversation next. As a coach, imagine yourself as having a third eye observing the conversation from the meta level and your awareness about the flow of the conversation. The answers you get will help you make the right decisions.

Meet up at the meta level

As mentioned, you will from time to time invite the coachee or team to join you at the meta level. The purpose for this is to have *a conversation about the conversation* to collaborate on designing the conversation, reflect on the learnings so far and make decisions about where to go next.

There are normally at least three opportunities for meeting at the meta level:

(1) When you are establishing a contract for the conversation
(2) When you are having a check-up during the conversation
(3) When you are concluding the conversation.

At the very start of the conversation, you should spend a little time on making contact with the one(s) you are coaching. Establishing contact helps people relax and feel confident in speaking freely. This is small talk and chit chat, talking about the weather, the traffic, how's-your-family, etc. Keep in mind that you should start

[3] The concept of powerful questions is explained up in sec. 3.6.

steering towards starting the actual coaching conversation before too long.

How you can establish the contract

When you are establishing the contract, you invite the other part to talk about the conversation you are about to have. The contract consists of an agreement that you will have a coaching conversation, the ground rules for the conversation and the goal for the conversation.

First of all, it should be clear for both parties that you are not just having a little chat. You are about to enter a serious conversation which might include both sensitive information and personal decisions. This expectation is sometimes implicit in the invitation, but it doesn't hurt to make it explicit. If you are in a discussion already and realize that it might turn into a coaching conversation, you might ask *"Is it OK if I ask you some questions to help you solve this problem?"* You can also set up a later meeting in a similar way: *"Should we sit down tomorrow and have a coaching conversation about this topic?"*

You will also need to establish the ground rules of the coaching conversation. This normally includes a statement of confidentiality from your side as well as the promise of an "emergency exit" for the coachee or individual team members. For confidentiality, we typically use the simple and strict Vegas Rule that we described earlier, in sec. 3.1. However, if the team you are coaching is large and the atmosphere in the organization is sufficiently constructive, forgiving and supporting, you could also consider the *Chatham House Rule*[4]. It states that all participants are free to use any information, but are not allowed to reveal who made any comment.

In recurring meetings the rules quickly become implicit and you don't need to repeat them, but when you are coaching someone

[4]https://www.chathamhouse.org/about/chatham-house-rule

for the first time you will have to explicitly set down the rules. We have a kind of boilerplate that we use that goes something like this:

"Before we get started, I would like to make it clear that I will keep this conversation confidential. I may bring up general issues with others, but won't talk about things that can be traced to you or to this discussion unless you give me permission. Also, you have the right to end the discussion and walk out if you feel like it, no questions asked. If at any point and for whatever reason you feel that you don't want to be in this room anymore, just say so and we will stop right there."

We find it good practice to have the counterpart formulate the goal of the conversation in one short sentence — and we usually also write it down in a notepad or on a sticky note. We usually ask questions like:

- *"What is the topic you want to elaborate and get insights on?"*
- *"How can I best serve you during this conversation?"*
- *"Are there questions you especially want me to ask or questions you absolutely do not want me to ask?"*
- *"When this conversation is over, where do you expect to be and what do you hope to have learned?"*

Now the actual coaching conversation can begin. Start by picking out keywords from the goals you just agreed on and formulate a question or several questions from that.

Having check-ups

During the conversation, you should from time to time make a timeout to check-up on the conversation. Look at the clock and the timebox, summarize the learning so far and decide where to go next.

Check-ups help to co-design the conversation on the fly with the purpose of bringing the most possible value into it. Think of it as a sort of in-sprint inspect-and-adapt cycle on the meta level.

You can use check-ups when you feel the conversation is at a crossroads in which you have to decide which path to take next. Be humble and unbiased: do not take for granted that your personal decision will be the best path. Instead ask the one(s) you are coaching what they think and follow their choice. Remember: it is not about you! It is all about them! You can also use check-ups to renegotiate the goal if you and the other person realize that another topic seems to be more important.

You can make as many check-ups as you feel necessary, asking questions like:

- *"Let me summarize the discussion so far. We have been discussing … and … , figuring out that … . Do you want to expand more on this, or would you rather move on and look at other options? What would that be?"*
- *"Let's look at where we are in this conversation. As I see it, we can either go in the direction of … or in the direction of … . You might see a third direction. Where do you want to go from here?"*
- *"Let's step out of the conversation and check how we are doing. In the beginning of this conversation we agreed to speak about … but it seems to me that we are now discussing … . What do you think, should we return to the original topic or is the new topic more important to you?"*

When the check-up is over you can continue the conversation taking into account the decisions you have just made together.

As an aside, we have found it useful to have a clock unobtrusively available. The simplest way is to put your wristwatch flat on the table beside your notepad. Smartwatches can be set to vibrate at certain points in time. Some smartphones can be configured to always show the time and there's a plethora of timer apps. If all else fails, simply explain that you want to see how much time is left before you pull out your phone or watch.

Define the next steps, starting with a clear conclusion

By the end of the conversation, it is time to come to a conclusion focusing on the specific steps the coachee or team is going to do, in order to initiate the desired change. Have him, her or them summarize the conclusion instead of you doing it. That fosters the sense of responsibility. Remember: it is not **your** solution — it is **their** solution!

As a follow up to the conversation, it is great practice to ask about what the next step will be, when this will be done and how you will know that this has been achieved. To the last question the one(s) you coach will usually answer something like: *"I'll send you an e-mail, letting you know how it went".* In service to the other part, you could then reply: *"And if I do not receive this mail, will it be helpful for you if I ask you about how it went?"* This attitude sharpens the awareness about the coaching conversation as something that serves a purpose, rather than just being a chat about life, the universe and everything.

End by asking for feedback

Finally, being a coach that wants to improve your skills, you should also ask for feedback about the coaching conversation. You can ask questions like: *"How was this conversation for you?", "What did I do that was especially useful for you?"* and *"Which questions did I ask that were useless or disturbing for your understanding of the matter?".*

Receive the feedback with gratitude and ask clarifying questions if you wish, but do not go into arguing about whether the feedback was right or wrong. You are asking for opinions and everyone is entitled to their own. The important matter is how the coachee or team experienced your coaching — there is most likely a point behind the feedback regardless of whether you liked it or not.

Just like you opened the conversation, it can also be good to close down the conversation with chit chat and small talk as you collect your pens and papers and pack your bag. If you are meeting the coachee or the team again, you might also want to agree on the time and perhaps a topic or even an agenda for your next meeting.

Try this

1) Coaching conversations are best practiced in a live setup. We recommend that you start out by practicing with individuals and once you are comfortable with this, you can move on to coaching teams. This means finding someone who is willing to be coached by you, even though you may still be a novice.

   Ideally the initial setup should be three persons: one who is coaching, one who is being coached (the coachee) and one who observes the conversation. This works very well if all three of you want to practice coaching. You can then take turns being the coach, the coachee and the observer. You can do 20-minute coaching conversations followed by five minutes of feedback from the observer, then take a five-minute break, switch roles and have a new coaching conversation. (Yes, as you probably already have figured out, the Pomodoro technique[5] can be used for many purposes.)

2) If you can't find an observer, then another option is to record the conversation and learn from it. You will of course need the permission of the coachee to record the conversation.

   Our experience tells us that while audio recordings are good, video recordings are much better for recall and understanding. Position the camera so that your upper body is in the

[5] See http://pomodorotechnique.com/

frame, not the coachee. Make sure that the picture is wide enough for you to move around, but still shows your postures and facial expressions clearly.

Most modern pocket cameras or smartphones are more than adequate for this purpose, but you may want to record a minute of video beforehand to extrapolate whether there is enough memory available. Downscale the video to a lower quality in order to save space, as low-quality video is better than no video at all. A cheap tripod, a fast charger and a long charging cable will also be useful.

3) Imagine a coaching conversation where you find it difficult to synchronize with the coachee. You can either think back to a previous coaching conversation that did not go as expected or think about an upcoming conversation with a person you are uncertain about.

   Now consider the communication enablers in sec. 3.4. Which ones were (or will be) especially relevant for the success of the conversation? Is there something related to the enablers that you could have done (or could now do) differently to improve the chances of success?

3.6 Powerful questions

"It is folly to say you know what is happening to other people. Only they know, if they exist. They have their own Universes of their own eyes and ears."
– Douglas Adams

Asking the right questions is a challenging task, especially when you do not want to impose your own opinion on to the person or team you are talking to. Great coaching questions are open-ended, non-judging and help foster new ideas and visions about possibilities. These kind of questions we call *powerful questions* (see fig. 3.4).

Figure 3.4: Powerful Questions

There are several approaches to creating powerful questions. They depend on which coaching school you are coming from. One approach is to practice a deck of questions until you know them by heart which helps you choose the right one in a given situation. Another approach is to learn a strategy for designing the right questions as needed. One such strategy that we have found works particularly well with both individuals and teams is based on a model developed by Canadian psychologist Karl Tomm.

The past and the future – simple and complex assumptions

The Karl Tomm approach has its roots in systemic theory. It encapsulates circularity and the understanding that each of us has a different perspective of the facts in a given situation and is entitled to that view. No one has monopoly on the truth; indeed different people can have very different perspectives and hence different understandings of what is happening and why.

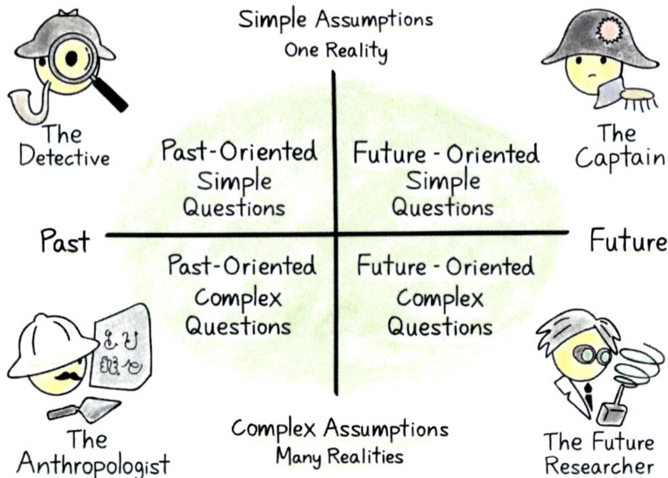

Figure 3.5: Karl Tomm's model for asking Powerful Questions

The model in fig. 3.5 shows two dimensions. Time is shown on the horizontal axis as *the past* and *the future*. On the vertical axis we can find *simple* (obvious, evident, linear) and *complex* (non-evident, multi-path, circular). While time should be easy to understand, the concept of simplicity vs. complexity may require a bit of explanation.

In a simple and linear world, there is little room for doubt. Cause-and-effect relations are easy to see and everybody can correctly predict the result of any given action. In the complex world, however, you generally can't draw a straight line from cause to effect. There can be multiple interacting causes, not all of them visible. There may also be circular cause-and-effect chains of different lengths, for example vicious loops and virtuous cycles. In a complex, circular world people may have quite different interpretations of why something happened the way it did, and sometimes even different opinions on what exactly happened.

Powerful questions are anchored in all four quadrants of Karl Tomm's model. The powerful questions can be aimed either at what has already happened (past-oriented), or at what could happen (future-oriented). The powerful questions can also be designed on the presumption that there is one and only one truth (linear questions) or so that they acknowledge the diversity in our understanding of the truth (circular questions).

When we ask questions that are past-oriented and linear (upper left in fig. 3.5), we ask questions like a detective in an interrogation, for example:

- *"What happened then?"*
- *"What kind of velocity did you have before that?"*
- *"When did it happen?"*
- *"How did it work out?"*
- *"Was it the PO or the customer?"*

As a detective, we are looking for facts that help us understand the issue. Remember that facts are undisputable: something either happened or it did not happen.[6] All kinds of data, statistics, recordings, diaries, blog posts, e-mails etc. are welcome.

But even when people are in the same place at the same time, they often end up with different observations. Memories have a tendency to evaporate over time. People fill in with assumptions when they don't have all the facts. This means that people can have very different interpretations of various events. Hidden assumptions are a major source of conflict and unearthing them can help immensely.

When we ask questions that are past-oriented and circular (lower left in the picture), we ask questions like an anthropologist doing

[6] As far as we know, this is the case everywhere except in Washington DC, where it might be helpful to explicitly say "a true fact".

research. We are looking for intentions and expanding our understanding of the intentions. For example, we could ask:

- *"What do you think was their motivation to do so?"*
- *"From which point of view could her action make sense?"*
- *"Could it be that they knew something that the rest of you did not? What could it be?"*
- *"Do you think she saw this as a problem at all?"*

Future-oriented circular questions (lower right) are intended to explore opportunities and different scenarios and expand possibilities. Here we ask questions like a future researcher, such as:

- *"What could you do to make things better?"*
- *"Is there something you could do to prevent this from happening in the future?"*
- *"Can you see a possible solution to this problem?"*

It can also be useful to apply appreciative inquiry and heliotropism to explore a positive and compelling future rather than focus on the problems and issues. One trick is to ask a "miracle question"; something that suggests that a miracle has happened overnight:

- *"If you come to work tomorrow and the problem has unexpectedly disappeared, how would you notice that?"*
- *"One day when you have solved this matter and look back on this period in time, which decisions did you make that made a difference?"*

Questions in this future-oriented, circular category might seem a bit strange at first, but give it a try. The advantage of questions like this is that they disconnect the person or team in front of you from the constrained situation they are currently in. They free up energy to see new perspectives and decide on new courses of action based on those perspectives. They help the person or team to see which part of the miracle or the desired future are already present today and how they can be used as stepping stones towards the goal.

Finally, we can ask simple or linear future-oriented questions (upper right). These are the kind of questions that a captain would ask. They are more direct and practical, defining the next steps for the desired change:

- *"What is the first thing you are going to do now?"*
- *"Who do you need to talk to in order to move this forward"*
- *"How can he or she help you?"*
- *"How will I know that you have done this?"*

Like at the end of a retrospective, this is where specific tasks are defined and prepared for action. As the coach your role is to ensure that the tasks are clear and simple, but also that the coachee takes responsibility. You can look back at sec. 3.5 for inspiration and more examples.

It is like driving a car

When coaching someone, we are mostly looking at the future and the change we are going to make. However, from time to time we must look back into the past to understand what has happened and why we are in the current situation. It is like driving a car; we are mostly looking out the windshield at the traffic in front of us, but from time to time we also need to look in the rear-view mirrors to know what is behind us.

There is no specific route you must follow when using Karl Tomm's discussion model. We have found that most of our coaching conversations tend to start in the detective dimension, moving on to the perspective of an anthropologist, then investigate as the future researcher and finally ending up as the captain. This is the order in which we introduced the quadrants in the previous section. You can imagine drawing the letter "U" over fig. 3.5, starting from the upper left. The path is not necessarily linear, though. On your way, you can jump back and forth as intuition tells you.

You have already learned about conversation flow, active listening and identifying keywords. You are now adding powerful questions to your toolbox of coaching skills. Asking powerful questions is a valuable coaching skill and one that can be improved with practice.

Critics are saying

When first exposed to powerful questions, your coachee or team members might think: *"What the heck is this guy up to?"* Especially if you are asking miracle questions. You may also personally feel a bit uncomfortable using these kind of questions. We recommend that you review your questions during and after the discussion, thinking back to which questions resulted in interesting and worthwhile answers and which questions seemed to break the flow or perhaps even offend the other person.

Especially questions from the anthropologist perspective are usually grounded in the belief that behind any action, there are good intentions.[7] Not everybody believes in this postulate and we must admit that we also regularly have to remind ourselves about it. Nevertheless, taking this approach will let you help people reflect as well as help solving conflicts.

You may also find it useful to remember that in any given situation, people try to do the best they can with the information and tools they have. We will return to the *Prime directive of retrospectives* by Norman Kerth in sec. 6.4.

[7] As stated by Humberto Maturana, one of the founders of the Systemic Theory.

While powerful questions are useful, they are not a silver bullet. For example, we sometimes run across teams that feel powerless, suppressed, oppressed or victimized. They may be stuck complaining about the past and refuse to move on to imagining a future. *"Yes, we tried something like that four years ago and it didn't work."* There are strategies for dealing with such teams, such as arranging a quick win in some area just to show that change can indeed happen or enlisting managers to help (although often the managers are part of the problem).

Try this

1. Think of a possible coaching situation. It can either be with a team or with a person one on one. It might be a coaching conversation you already had with someone or you may be preparing for an upcoming coaching situation.

   Try walking around in the Karl Tomm model and formulate questions from the four different perspectives. Formulate at least three questions in each dimension. You might have to imagine the answers you will get in order to formulate new questions.

   Next, practice asking powerful questions in live coaching situations. You can also use them in situations you would not normally consider to be coaching situations, like in Daily Scrum for example.

2. When you are in a suitable coaching conversation, spend some extra effort at the beginning of the conversation separating facts from interpretations. Write statements and keywords on stickies and put them on a Karl Tomm model on a whiteboard. Ask questions that help you understand whether a statement is a fact or an assumption and recategorize the stickies as necessary.

   "The PO moved a difficult backlog item from their backlog to ours" is a fact, while *"the PO did it because he thinks the other*

team doesn't like difficult backlog items" would be an interpretation.

Chapter 4

Coaching conversations with a team

In the previous chapters, we covered the basics of systemic coaching, such as how to listen and keep a conversation flowing without actually steering it; how to open up a new coaching conversation and guide it to closure; and how to formulate questions so that the coachee provides the content while you provide the structure. As you start getting the feel for how to run coaching conversations with individuals, you can move on to having coaching conversations with teams.

Coaching teams is far more complex than coaching individuals. You probably already have guessed that. When coaching a whole team, you need to focus on more than one person; you need to be aware of the perspectives and intentions of several people; and you need to master both steering the conversation towards a goal, letting each of them have airtime and help the team finding consensus. Tough job, isn't it?

Well, *Don't Panic*, even though the going gets tough. In this chapter, we will introduce you to some tools and techniques that you can use in team conversations.

4.1 Bridging questions

While the *powerful questions* we discussed in the previous section are useful for "opening the box" and creating progression throughout a discussion, the intention of *bridging questions* is to collect

Figure 4.1: Bridging questions

thoughts and ideas and to build a common understanding in the team.

In team coaching conversations, bridging questions gather information and conclusions and help the team find and expand on a common agreement. They build, so to speak, a bridge between the different team members' attitudes, experiences, opinions and suggestions. They bring out new information and help resolve conflicts.

Your ability to use bridging questions is the first step towards mastery of team coaching conversations.

The idea behind Bridging Questions

One of the the major challenges in newly formed teams is making decisions. Good decisions require the right amounts of exploration, dissent, analysis and effort. Some teams can take a very long time to get this right.

There are several ways in which the decision-making process can go wrong. One common issue is that the team starts digging into the first reasonable solution instead of exploring options, thereby limiting their solution space. People can sometimes take criticism of an idea very personally and start defending that idea beyond what is reasonable. Another common problem occurs when two or more persons each have individual agendas to drive. Having a strong opinion and being vocal about it doesn't mean that the opinion is the best.

As a great team coach, you must ensure that all members take part in the conversation and contribute to the solution. Through the use of bridging questions, you can create strong links between the team members by linking the ideas generated by them. You do this by formulating questions that nudge team members into relating their answers to what was previously said by others, instead of just pursuing their own agenda. Some examples:

- *"What similarities do you see in what different people are saying here?"*
- *"In what way do the things Paul is speaking about link to your interest in the subject? What can you add to this?"*
- *"In what way are you inspired when you hear the others discuss the subject?"*
- *"Is there something you feel that the others have forgotten in their discussion?"*
- *"In which way can you see that your thoughts are aligned with other people's opinions? In which way do your thoughts differ from the others' opinions?"*

For example, we once encountered a team with a very respected, skilled and resourceful developer who was also a strong open source advocate. His pet feature was to maintain compatibility with a similar open source project, even though this played no role in the company's strategy. He would inject backlog items and add tasks related to this project (e.g. "Maintain compatibility with XML schema changes in OSS project") and while the team grumbled a little they did not speak out. The PO did not have enough technical knowledge to see what was happening.

By the use of bridging questions, we made him aware that most people on the team did not enjoy the extra work and in fact thought it a bit silly. After a few rounds of this he came to the conclusion that it was time to drop the topic. As a result the team became more focused and their throughput increased markedly to the happy surprise of the PO.[1]

We have also seen teams where people don't respond much to bridging questions, saying things like "I don't know," or "Nothing comes to mind." Sometimes they are just indifferent, sometimes afraid of rocking the boat, and sometimes they are genuinely unable to come up with anything. This could indicate that you are working with a workgroup or pseudo-team that lacks synergy and heedfulness, something we will discuss further in sec. 5. But there are also ways of creating peer pressure within a discussion by drawing on people's feelings and emotions. In the next section we will explain how you can do that.

Reflecting participants

Some team members might not have a strong opinion about a certain topic, so they might choose to be passive in a team discussion and let two or three strong minded members drive their own arguments. This has several problems. Since some of the expertise now

[1] We also like open source software but we think focus is more important.

lies latent, the team risks reaching a premature conclusion and the passive team members are not helping resolve the conflicts either.

A great team coach can invite the passive participants into the conversation by asking them to reflect on what the strong-minded members have said:

- *"What do you especially like about the ideas of Peter? Paul? and Mary?"*
- *"When Peter and Paul are arguing so strongly for each of their different opinions, which similarities do you see in their opinions that they might not see?"*

A reflecting participant can also provide a strong contribution for solving a conflict:

- *"When you experience that Paul and Mary are having this conflict, how does it make you feel? How do you think the others feel?"*

This approach relies on the fact that people are social animals and as such reluctant to upset others in the "tribe". People who keep distressing or angering others are generally going to be pushed towards the fringe of the social group.[2] In prehistoric times this would have a negative impact on your chances of surviving and finding a mate and thus the asocial tendencies would mostly be bred out of the population.

In modern times, people often belong to multiple "tribes", either permanently or for a shorter time. This could include family, childhood friends, old classmates, neighbours, hobbyist groups, various fan clubs and, of course, teams at work. As coaches, we can exploit the social glue in a workgroup to help the group come to a joint conclusion in the way we just outlined above.

[2]Watch out for bullies, narcissists and other sociopaths. They instead form the core of such groupings and survive by exploiting this tendency in others.

4.2 The 5D model

Back in sec. 3.6, we looked at Karl Tomm's approach as a way of generating powerful questions. We can also look at it as a complete path through a team coaching conversation. We would apply the coaching conversation structure from sec. 3.5, keep the discussion flowing using active listening and use the powerful questions to create a coherent direction in the discussion.

This approach works well enough for us to use it as the "default" in many coaching conversations. It works especially well in situations of conflict, because a large part of the discussion is spent on discovering facts together and creating a common understanding that includes different interpretations. It also works well if the team is aware of some pain point, but cannot formulate what it is.

However, while Karl Tomm's model is good at digging into the past, it is not as good at dreaming up ambitious goals. In this section we would like to introduce another path through a coaching conversation that we call the 5D Model. The 5D model helps the team choose or formulate the problem to be addressed; share past experiences that might be worth trying; explore what a great solution could look like; define the stepping stones towards this solution; and decide who is doing what. It can be especially useful if the team has found a problem that they want to solve either in an ad hoc discussion or in a separate retrospective meeting.

The 5D Model, shown in fig. 4.2, is rooted in appreciative inquiry that we mentioned briefly in sec. 3.2. It consists of five phases: Define, Discover, Dream, Design and Deliver. You can run this as a guided discussion, or you can plan exercises to draw out the best ideas.

Define

In this phase, we define the topic we would like to develop in this coaching conversation. This phase is somewhat similar to

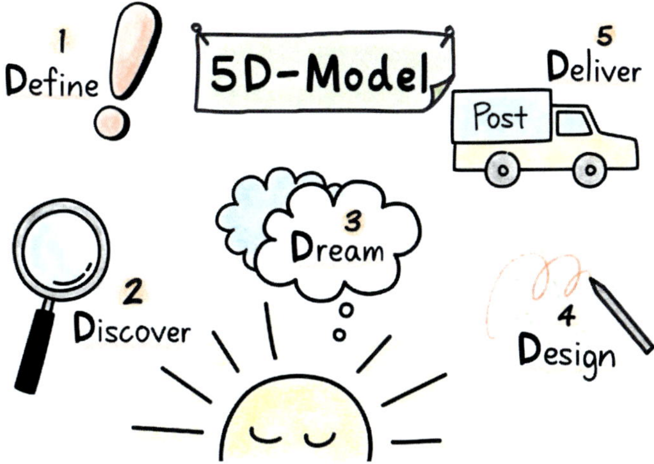

Figure 4.2: The 5D Coaching Model

establishing the contract in a classic coaching conversation. We describe the development area through "transforming questions" — questions that have a special power of change designed in. In contrast to problem-solving questions, transforming questions are constructive and positive and focus on the goal rather than the problem, as illustrated by the following example:

- Problem-solving question: *"How do we prevent our meetings from being so boring and unimportant?"*
- Transforming question: *"How do we create dedicated meetings that help us realize the improvements we have set as goal?"*

As you can see, the basic principle here is to base the questions on the situation that you want to achieve rather than the situation you want to avoid. Problem-solving questions are not wrong as such, but they can drain the energy from the team. In our experience, team coaching discussions benefit from “dreaming big”. Be ambitious and stretch this goal by making it lofty, so that the questions will give constructive leverage later in the conversation.

Discover

In this phase, you explore the past experiences of the team members with a focus on successful events and incidents. The purpose is to describe and explain the contexts that illustrates the best practice of the team members. It is important that the questions are as specific as possible.

Because the team is focusing on the things where they have succeeded, we are already fostering the positive effect of the problem solving in this phase. If the team has little or no prior positive experiences related to the topic, ask the team members to think of other teams that have succeeded in similar situations. This can include teams that some of the members have been a part of in the past or neighbouring teams in the same company or competing companies or perhaps something from a book or article.

As a coach, you can use multiple tools to facilitate and drive the workshop. If you run this as a discussion, remember to regularly sum up the experiences the team is talking about. You can also facilitate a Brainstorming exercise with stickies, or the Brainwriting variant that also activates silent members. If the group is large (15+ people) you could run a quick World Café.

You can also split the team and give the groups different targets, e.g. one group to ideate and list mainstream ideas; one to work on the loftiest, most inspiring ideas; one to come up with the weirdest possible ideas; one on anti-ideas (ones that prevent you from achieving your goal); and so on. Make presentations or a gallery walk at the end to spread the knowledge around.

Dream

Having a common picture of the ideal situation for the team in the foreseeable future is a very powerful tool. It helps the team keep on track as they are improving. Here the focus is on the future and the team's desire for ideal practices or an ideal situation. If "dreaming of the perfect future" feels too fuzzy or idealistic, you can instead use terms like "vision" or "ideas".

At this stage, you should strive to create a playful and welcoming atmosphere — a "*yes, and*" mindset — so that team members gradually become bolder as they experience the friendly welcome of their ideas and imaginations. It is therefore important to avoid negative replies or rejection of a team member. Instead draw inspiration and build on top of the ideas of others, providing more details and offshoots of each other's imaginations. All ideas are welcome.

With minor changes, many tools from the Discover phase also work well in the Dream phase. If you facilitate a conversation, try using bridging questions to build a common understanding. You can also have multiple groups work on different perspectives on the same issue (for example People/Process/Product) and merge their results. You can also try the Park Bench or Fish Bowl exercises.

Design

Based on the wishes for the future and the best experiences of the past, we now examine which of the possible future situations will be of particular relevance to the team. We help the team define what approach or approaches they should focus on. Again, it is important to keep the wording as concrete and action-oriented as possible.

Deliver

In this final phase, the goal is to define the actions and plans of action to achieve the objectives. The responsibility is defined, so it is clear to everybody who is doing what and when. This clarification should be explicit and detailed, so no one is in doubt about his or her role in the near future. It should also be agreed about when to follow up, so the implementation can be secured and supported. The concept of SMART actions[3] can be helpful.

Sometimes we find that teams are nervous about going forward with the concepts they have Dreamed and Designed. The concepts look good on paper, but reality strikes when they start drawing up concrete action plans. Throughout the Design and Deliver phases, keep an eye open for uncertainty. For example, we have found it useful to ask the team members to individually judge how sure they are about the proposal. We ask them to think of a number from 0 to 10, where ten means absolute certainty and zero means that they really can't say anything, then raise that number of fingers.

If it turns out that the team feels generally uncertain about the proposal, ask them what would increase the score. If there are different opinions in the team, ask what makes people sure and what makes them unsure. If they still feel uncertain, help them create time-limited safe-to-fail experiments. The outcome of the actions will then be learning and knowledge.

The 5D model is a powerful and effective communication structure because it breaks the way we usually think of improvements. By anchoring the discussion in *what has actually worked* instead of what does not work, we can increase motivation and enthusiasm and pave the way for future learnings.

The model does put a lot of responsibility on the facilitator, though. As you will notice, guiding the team through the model takes some

[3]SMART = Specific, Measurable, Achievable, Relevant and Timely. See http://en.wikipedia.org/wiki/SMART_criteria

careful balancing between guarded optimism and, well, *unguarded* optimism. The "landing curve" from Dream into Delivery can be tricky, especially if the team you are coaching has been conditioned over the years not to rock the boat. Make sure to help them out: talk to the managers; drop some words in the right places; bring the stakeholders' attention to the right issues.

4.3 Try this

1) Reflect on the benefit of bridging questions — how can you see yourself using them in practice? Formulate one or two bridging questions that you can use in general. Memorize them and try them out when you have the next opportunity to do so.

2) Think about an upcoming discussion where there might be an argument between two or more people. This might be a retrospective or perhaps a backlog refinement or sprint planning meeting, where you know that people will promote different approaches.

   Who of the other participants could you involve through a bridging question? (If there are none, you may want to invite a couple of peers, for example.) Prepare a couple of bridging questions aimed at different people. Write the questions down, then try them out in the meeting.

3) The Karl Tomm and 5D models are best practiced when you have an actual open conversation with a team, for example in a retrospective.

   Prepare by drawing one of the models on a flip-chart (look at fig. 3.5 or fig. 4.2 for the general layouts) and reflect on which questions you could ask the team in each of the phases.

Bring the flip-chart to the retrospective, give the team a short introduction to the model and use it during your conversations. Document your journey through the model by writing stickies and putting them on the flip-chart. Point out to the team whenever you change phase in the model.

Chapter 5

Team dynamics

Information systems today (and indeed the last 50+ years) are just too large for one single software engineer to handle. Even though we have excellent building blocks in the form of stable, low-cost software stacks — operating systems, standard libraries, databases, etc. — it turns out that we need a whole team and often several teams to get stuff done in a reasonable time, before the customer grows tired or the market moves on.

Having more people around brings a number of positive side effects. More people means more ideas and this gives us a wider source of potential solutions. Team members can become sparring partners, helping each other improve in their craft and reviewing each others work to improve the quality. The team can, as a whole, cover a larger experience and expertise area than any one single developer and they also have better opportunities to share and spread the workload.

But teams can also suffer from communication and synchronization problems. The more people and roles you have, the longer it takes for information to disseminate and decisions to be made. Some people find it difficult to work together. There are egos that need satisfaction and people who drive their own agendas. Teamwork does not happen by itself.

In our experience, successfully adopting the mechanics of Scrum will generally give any workgroup a 15–30 % increase in productivity. This comes from focusing on the content (delivering running tested software) rather than the container (project plans, work breakdown structures, gantt charts, hourly reports, bug statistics).

Basically, the team starts doing the right things and doing them right.

From a traditional perspective, a 15 % increase in productivity is simply incredible. A traditional manager would kill for that kind of improvement! But those teams are still lacking synergy. By carefully nurturing your team past the initial formation stage, by letting them collaborate and gain trust and start demanding mutual accountability, you can grow a high-performance team. Even in strictly traditional organizations where Scrum and Kanban are seen as some kind of weird process used only in R&D, we find teams that continue to ramp up productivity by 20–50 % year after year.

Again, this does not happen by itself. It requires a dedicated line manager, a skilled Product Owner, an effective ScrumMaster and, of course, a team that is willing and allowed to rise to the challenge. In this chapter we will explore the concept of groups, pseudo-teams and high-performing teams and how you, as a coach, can help people move them from one to the other.

5.1 Synergy in teams

In the movie “Cast Away”, Tom Hanks plays the character of Chuck Noland. As the title implies, Chuck is stranded on a desert island. But he is not alone: he has a companion, Wilson, in the form of a volleyball! Unfortunately, Wilson is of the silent type and does not offer much help. Even though Chuck is very resourceful and innovative — he extracts a bad tooth with a skate, among other things — he is never able to achieve more than his own effort and ingenuity can provide. Chuck Noland is solely one man, not a team.

What if we have several people? A group of people, for example, standing at a bus stop, still can not achieve more than the sum of the effort from each person. In a working group, people typically have a professional relationship and exchange information related to their work, but they do this only in order to achieve their individual goals. People at a bus stop exchange information about when the next bus will arrive, but will use this information to optimize their own journey and use of time, sometimes to the point of competing for the limited space in the bus. A working group lacks synergy.

At the other extreme, a Formula One team running a pit stop is a great example of synergy. Their shared goal is to win the grand prix and in order to do that they need to get a top position in the race today. Thus their immediate target is to get the F1 car out of the pit stop as quickly as humanly possible. Because of this shared goal, as well as having agreed on roles and procedures, they are able to achieve more than if they were working as individuals in a group. Everyone in the team collaborates to get the car moving again. The team consists of experts, not specialists. (A specialist only specializes in one thing, while an expert can have expertise in many areas.) If a team member is having problems, others will step in and help. It doesn't matter who does the job as long as it gets done quickly and efficiently.

The difference between a team and a working group is *synergy*. Individuals can't achieve synergy for the obvious reasons. Groups don't have synergy by definition. Only when a group has worked together towards a shared goal for long enough to jell together can we call them a high-performing team. But what is this "jelling"? How do you recognize it? And how do you make it happen?

We would like to refer to an important article by Weick and Roberts (1993). As they studied teams that perform well in challenging environments, they noted that the synergistic effects are born in *interpretations and actions.* Team members contribute to the goals by acting according to their own interpretations of the situation and recent events. Obviously if team members have different understandings of the situation and the goal, no synergy is possible. But if their interpretations are aligned so that they support and

Figure 5.1: Synergy in teams

supplement each other, then the contributing actions will also converge and give synergistic effects. The whole collective activity system of habits, actions, signals and reactions becomes greater than the sum of its parts.

For example, one team that we coached dug up an old Nabaztag[1] and hacked it so that for each commit, it would run different kinds of static and dynamic analysis on the new code and then publicly announce what it thought of it. If the rabbit gave negative feedback, other team members would tease the hapless author but then generally help her out. Soon people started to confer with others or work in pairs before committing code, in order to get kudos from the "Killer Rabbit". What started as a nifty hack

[1] An internet-connected plastic rabbit with ears that could be rotated remotely. Yes, you read that correctly. Look it up.

became a cornerstone in the team's attempt to strengthen the habit of writing good code.

Weick and Roberts note that this kind of social intelligence requires a certain level of *heed* in the group members. Heedful people are attentive, observant, careful, respectful and helpful towards others. The more heedfulness in the system, the more developed the collective mind will be. It can even transcend the individuals, meaning that the patterns and habits remain when individuals come and go. When members start acting out of habit or relying on luck, some of the collective intelligence is lost and performance degrades.

From the perspective of agile coaching, the most important concept in the whole article is that one can strengthen and renew the heedful interpretation and contribution patterns that form the collective mind. Weick and Roberts note that heedful teams tend to:

- Make the patterns visible
- Model and discuss them
- Reward reinforcing actions
- Preserve anecdotes

Agile teams use working agreements, a Definition of Done, team boards, team signals, information radiators, zero defect tolerance, build scripts etc. etc. to make things visible. As an agile coach, you are in a unique position to help them out in the daily standups and retrospectives. You can teach them concepts like visual management and automation, and facilitate meaningful conversations about what they see.

Of the surrounding roles, the ScrumMaster and the line manager are best positioned to see reinforcing actions and give rewards. In the "Killer Rabbit" case we mentioned above, the ScrumMaster was the one to drop the initial idea and the line manager was instrumental in helping the team find a solution that was compliant with the IT security guidelines.

The same people can also help the team form a collective history. A scratched snowboard carefully leaning against an old server or a dusty, unopened magnum champagne bottle with an equally dusty and unopened congratulatory card are each telling their separate stories. If this sounds like team identity and culture… it is. If it sounds like it will be difficult in a distributed team… you're right, again.

5.2 Team development and performance models

Team forming and performance does not happen by itself. You cannot form a team by placing 5–9 persons in a room and shouting "SELF-ORGANIZE!" as you close the door.

Given a moderately healthy environment and time to work together, a group of people will generally start collaborating to achieve better performance. This can take a long time, however, and not all groups will get there in the end. There might be incompatible personalities or people who simply do not get along. A skilled coach can guide groups past the worst pitfalls and help them build a well-performing team much faster than they could do it on their own.

In the 1960's, Bruce Tuckman (1965) introduced a model for understanding the development of teams. The model is interesting for agile coaches, because if we can identify the stage of the team, then we can determine what interactions with the team would be appropriate. The model in its original form consists of four stages:

Forming — Group members are generally attentive and well-behaved, but self-focused. The group of people is looking for answers on questions like: Who is in the team? What are we expected to do? How shall we do it? Who are we reporting to?

Here the agile coach should help the team members to get to know each other and clarify the basic terms, objectives, vision and values. Assuming that these remain stable, the team should move into Storming on their own.

Storming — The group members are starting to form opinions about each other. They are trying to establish a common understanding of the goals, roles and procedures, but have challenges coordinating and resolving difficulties.

Here the agile coach should work on diversity, dissent and conflict resolution/dissolution. In other words, it is OK to have differing opinions, but people need to learn how to constructively build on top of the contributions of others.

Use bridging questions (see sec. 4.1) to help people understand what others are thinking. Team building exercises can be very useful at this stage and you could use exercises such as the Market of Skills and Skills Matrix to help the team see what kind of people the others are.

Norming — Members are starting to understand and accept the different working habits in the team. The team starts establishing a common understanding, roles and procedures through self assessment and agreements. The community will be established and each individual will begin to accommodate herself.

Here the agile coach should encourage the development of the team-specific common understandings, roles, routines, etc. Help the team create working agreements, coding guidelines and pull policies. Update the Definition of Done and streamline the task board. Help the team build their identity: pick a team name; encourage some fun and silliness; retain souvenirs; let them rearrange their corner of the office; help them set up their own information radiators; etc.

Performing — A team in this stage can primarily concentrate on getting the job done, rather than thinking about procedures, cooperation and organizing. The cooperation is working well and there is less talk about process and self assessment.

Here the ScrumMaster or agile coach should help encourage work performance through a focus on excellence, further potentials, new goals and targets, etc.

Note that this stage is very wide and doesn't account for the presence (or lack) of synergy. It covers all working groups and teams that have established their roles and procedures and are now focusing mainly on the actual work. The performance can be low or high or anything in between.

Teams do not necessarily progress linearly through the model. Tuckman noted that many teams skip the Storming stage altogether, going directly from Forming to Norming. Other teams can get stuck in Storming or Norming. And whenever the team setup changes (members leave or join) or the context changes (the team relocates or is transferred to another department), the team becomes a little less mature. It can, for example, drop from Performing back to Norming or even all the way to Forming. The agile coach should change her interactions to reflect this new situation.

Research of team performance conducted by Jon Katzenbach and Douglas Smith and described in their iconic book *The Wisdom of Teams* (Katzenbach and Smith, 1993), shows how the performance of a team is impacted when a group of people develops from being a working group to a high-performance team. Katzenbach and Smith describe the following stages, also shown in fig. 5.2:

Working group — A working group is merely a group of people, for which group performance is primarily dependent on individual contributions. The working group is the sum of its parts but nothing more and there is little potential for improvement.

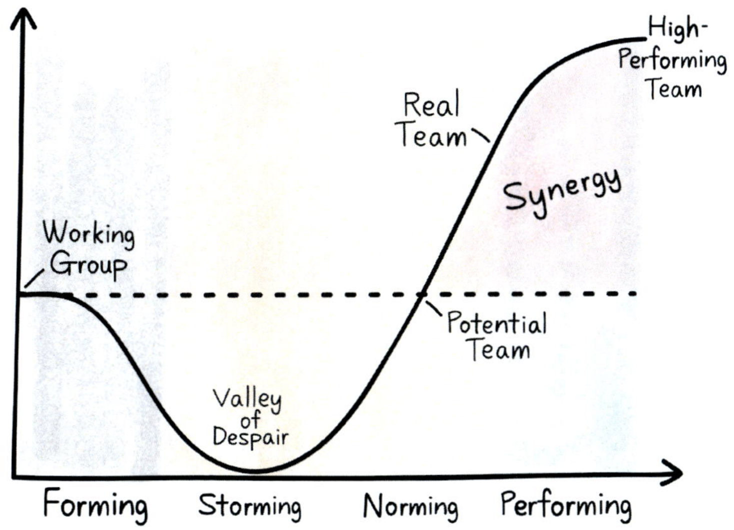

Figure 5.2: Team performance

Members do not take responsibility for results other than their own, nor do they try to develop incremental performance contributions requiring the combined, real work of two or more group members. In other words, there is no synergy in the working group.

Pseudo-team — This is a working group for which there could be a significant, incremental performance need or opportunity, but the group either does not recognize this potential or is not interested or capable of working towards it. The typical pseudo-team is not focused on collective performance and is not trying to achieve it.

It can be very discouraging to be part of a pseudo-team where the members are not interested in jelling. This can sometimes lead to a vicious cycle of mediocrity and stress, an ongoing state of low productivity that we call the Valley of Despair (see the end of sec. 5.3 for more information).

When coaching a working group or a pseudo-team, you should focus on fostering a team identity. Help them create a common goal and also introduce opportunistic collaboration where it makes sense. Show them that collaboration can be fun and profitable individually (learning) as well as collectively (quality, performance). Also help them visualize their work and understand what is happening.

Potential team — This is a group with a significant, incremental performance need that is interested in improving its performance and is actively working to achieve this. Typically, the group would need more clarity about purpose, goals or work products and more discipline in hammering out a common working approach. It has not yet established collective accountability.

When coaching a potential team, show them how easy it is to try out new techniques and working methods. Focus on improving the retrospectives and ensure that the team is in control of its working agreements, tools and processes. Ensure that they have simple but good metrics with both leading and lagging indicators so that they know when they are improving.

Real team — This is a small number of people with complementary skills who are equally committed to a common purpose, goals and working approach for which they hold themselves mutually accountable.

In order to become a high-performing team, the team needs to set up personal professional development plans together. They will also need to know how to give and take feedback. As a coach, you can help them achieve this.

High-performing team — This is a group that meets all the conditions of a real team. In addition, the members are deeply committed to one another's personal growth and success and new members will also join this commitment. The high-performing team significantly outperforms all other similar teams and also outperforms all reasonable expectations given its membership. In the performing phase the team has reached synergy and are getting a lot more out of their individual contributions.

We would like to mention that we especially like the Market of Skills team exercise, as it contains many components that are important for teams in the early Tuckman and Katzenbach-Smith stages. This is something we try to introduce in all teams that have worked together for less than a year. As a follow-up, the Skills Matrix helps people see collaboration opportunities, which is essential in pseudo-teams as well as potential teams.

The Tuckman and Katzenbach-Smith models look very similar and we chose to draw them as parallel tracks in fig. 5.2. This is not always the case. One could argue that the Katzenbach-Smith model continues where the Tuckman model stops (with a bit of overlap). A forming or storming team according to Tuckman can at most be a potential team in the Katzenbach-Smith model and what Tuckman considers a performing team may still be only a pseudo-team according to Katzenbach-Smith.

Furthermore, the Tuckman model is team-internal only and team formation can be strengthened regardless of the organization (assuming of course that the budding team is not torn apart all the time). Improvements along the Katzenbach-Smith model are, however, strongly dependent on the surrounding organization and require understanding and support from the ScrumMaster, PO, line manager and stakeholders. For example, if the line manager keeps using new words but acts like always before, the team will notice this.

Becoming a real team requires that each member is willing to take risks and trust the others. Where they previously had individual actions and separate work products, they will now have collective actions and joint work products. They need to agree on a common purpose, set goals, decide on the approach, and take mutual accountability. There will be conflicts that need to be handled in constructive ways. People who call themselves teams but take no such risks are at best pseudo-teams.

5.3 Challenges in forming teams

As we mentioned earlier, teams do not "happen" by themselves. Even assuming that the different personalities on the team can get along, there can be multiple stumbling blocks along the way. According to the book "Effective Teamwork" (West, 2012), there are several challenges in forming teams, including:

Free-riding — Free-riding can happen when someone realizes that his or her personal effort is no longer visible. With half a dozen other people doing hard work, nobody will notice if one person just "floats along", right?

This was first described by Maximilien Ringelmann (1913) through a simple experiment in a rope pulling contest. When the test person is told that he has six strong firemen on his team, he will pull less than if he believed he was one of the strongest. Ringelmann also found that the individual involvement decreases in larger groups.

Inefficient decision-making — Team decisions are hard to make. Team decisions are usually better than the average individual decisions made by the team members, but worse than a decision made by the most brilliant team member. Team decisions are highly influenced by the persons who speak first and loudest within the team. These may be people who want individual recognition or promotion or managers who want the team to come to a specific decision. There are many tools to reduce this influence, such as Roman Voting, Fist of Five and Planning Poker.

Hogging credit — In a well-working team, the team as a whole takes responsibility for successes as well as failures. The road there can be bumpy, however. Individual contributors can find it very challenging to trust other persons on the team if it can influence their own personal standing in the company.

In this context, hogging credit means to make sure that your own role in a success is emphasized or exaggerated ("Looks like the architecture I drew up served us quite well"), while distancing yourself from failure ("I said we should check it with the customer, but they didn't listen"). Credit-hogging can happen in private discussions as well as in public communications. It is often subtle and difficult to disprove, except to those who see it first hand: the team-mates.

The challenges listed above are all *internal* to the team. But there are also *external* challenges. Many organizations are, in fact, set up in a way that undermines or outright prevents the formation of high-performing teams. Some factors include:

Deep specialization — A specialist has deep knowledge in one area, which is usually quite narrow. Specialists are not rewarded for helping others and can be reprimanded if they try. Therefore, they have a tendency to focus on their own narrow area and are not used to collaborating.

Specialization is a good survival strategy in mechanistically designed organizations and many managers are proud of the depth of knowledge in their teams.

As a coach, you will need to make people understand that being a generalist or expert (in many different areas) is an even better survival strategy. Both the organization and the individual will benefit from having a wider profile of skills.

Belief in heroism — When a project is behind schedule, managers often try to create more work hours per day. Engineers get to spend long evenings and weekends at the office. Othertimes strict processes and decision hierarchies force people to bypass processes and do work under the radar in order to get things done in a reasonable time.

To make up for it, managers reward these just-get-it-done people with public recognition, gifts and bonuses, sending everyone the message that heroism is highly valued. In the end, the whole organization believes that working overtime or bypassing processes is normal.

A coach would need to promote strict timeboxes or WIP limits, as well as sustainable development and team accountability, in order to expose the danger with heroism.

Lack of transparency — In centrally directed organizations, information often flows from the operative layers inwards or upwards, while the outwards or downwards flow consists mainly of decisions. Information may even be withheld from operative personnel by the central layers.

Lacking broader information, people are unable to make good decisions and will instead push their own opinions and agendas. In those kind of systems, politicians who talk smoothly and know what information to share with whom will prosper. Central systems are also slow to respond, although they are good at retaining standardization.

Creating visibility and transparency is important. Presenting work progress in a central obeya (war room) can be very useful, especially if managers start using that room as a base for making decisions.

Individual incentives — Personal bonus plans make people work for their own profit rather than for what's best for the whole company. For example, a developer may decline to help a teammate with a project-related problem because that project is not on her incentive plan. Another typical example is that a salesman sells a new feature that turns out to be technically very challenging to implement.

We have found that replacing individual incentives with team incentives helps a lot. It is also a good idea to base incentives on actual outcomes and make them win-wins rather than guesswork-based metrics: "Deliver as quickly and cheaply as possible" rather than "Deliver by Oct 15 and at a cost of maximum 1.2 million." We have seen that relative targets work better than absolute metrics: "Improve the lead time by 15 %" rather than "Reach a lead time of 8 days."

Salary discrepancies — In many companies, salaries are set on an individual basis. This means that people are in fact rewarded for negotiation skills rather than technical and teamworking skills and for changing jobs rather than staying with their teams. Managers may also be handcuffed by a limited increases budget, creating a situation where employees have to compete with each other for a raise. This is obviously a problem for managers as well as for employees.

Changing an existing wage system inside a large corporation is going to be very difficult. Managers may find opportunities when setting up new teams from scratch. Many agile companies still retain opaque wages. There are also companies with transparent wage systems. For more insights you may, for example, want to read "Joy, Inc." by Richard Sheridan (2013).

Status rewards — Where wage discrepancies are often kept secret, status rewards are more or less public. This can include such things as a personal corner office, a standing authorization to travel first class, a named parking place... or ownership of a red stapler. They may start out as reasonable allowances or have some historic background, but eventually take on a life of their own and become a source of friction between people.

Agile companies take the status rewards off the table by making the same rewards available to all employees. In cases where supply is indeed limited, shared resource pools with usage transparency usually work fine.

Mandated corporate tools — While tools can be very useful, we find that they can also cause unintended negative behavior. For example, if your tool automatically assigns an owner to every backlog item or task, it could cause team members to focus more on their own tasks and thereby collaborate less. A tool that uses the term "requirement" instead of "backlog item" could increase the threshold for proposing changes. And a cumbersome tool with strict access control might result in backlogs not being updated in a timely manner.

To fix this you can try to find a reasonable compromise. For example, many teams maintain control of their work by moving the smallest level of detail (tasks that are measured in hours) out of the tool and on to a physical task board. They move post-its on a daily basis and update the larger-scale items in the corporate tool when necessary.

Project resourcing — One particularly common problem is project resourcing, meaning the way teams are routinely disbanded after a project and reassembled with different people for the next project. The reason is that a team needs to invest time and effort in becoming a high-performing team. Both the Tuckman and Katzenbach-Smith models assume that the group of people is stable for long enough to make this investment.

On the way to high performance, the team must go through the Valley of Despair (see fig. 5.2), where much of the effort is spent on establishing the pecking order and coping with dissent and where their productivity is even worse than it was at the start. Getting beyond this can take a long time. The normal timespan from starting out as a working group to becoming a high-performing team is between six to twelve months.

Whenever you disband and re-form teams, they lose everything they have invested in bonding and jelling with their team mates. Over time they learn that the process is not even worth starting. There is instead a high risk that they take permanent residence in the Valley of Despair. This is not a great place to be. Unfortunately, many organizations are unaware of the magnitude of the problem as they have no stable and high-performing teams to compare against.

5.4 Summary

In this chapter, we discussed how teams differ from workgroups and we covered several different models for forming and developing teams and for identifying and avoiding common pitfalls. Team synergy and building up trust are so important that an agile coaching engagement can be considered an exercise in team building.

An agile coach continuously observes how people behave within the system and tries to change the system so that people can change their behavior for the better. In sec. 7 we will look at a structured method for improving teams.

5.5 Try this

1) Choose a team you are working with. Observe the team members both as individuals and as a group and assess the team using the Tuckman and Katzenbach-Smith models.

Next, choose an exercise, a work habit or a topic to raise that may help the team move on to the next stage. Validate your chain of reasoning with the ScrumMaster, the Product Owner, the development manager, and other stakeholders surrounding the team. Apply it and reflect on the results.

2) Observe a team you are currently working with. Which of the challenges listed in sec. 5.3 are most prominent in the team? Why do they occur?

Chapter 6

Coaching your team

By now we have covered what agile coaching is, talked about how to structure and facilitate coaching discussions with individuals and teams, discussed how groups of individuals can develop into teams, and how to form a new agile team. Next up, we will cover some of the better-known agile and lean frameworks and think about how they support agile coaching.

Figure 6.1: Inspect and adapt

You will be coaching the team every time you meet them, but there are subtle differences in what to focus on in the different meetings and events. During backlog refinement and sprint planning meetings, you should focus on facilitating — helping the team and stakeholders make great product decisions. After the daily standups, however, you have a great opportunity to grab five or ten minutes with the team following up on how they are doing short term. In the retrospectives, you can drive long term team questions.

6.1 What is built into your framework?

The framework you have chosen supports coaching in certain ways. Scrum conveniently provides a number of pre-scheduled meetings and touch points with the team, so there is little to plan.

Scrum also has two specific roles besides the development team, namely the ScrumMaster and the Product Owner. Both of these are make and break roles. As the agile coach, your job will become difficult and you will lose precious time if one of the designated persons is unsuitable for the job or doesn't have enough time to do it well.

Kanban, on the other hand, doesn't define any meetings or roles. We find that many teams pick up meetings from other agile methods and these generally fall in one of three categories:

1. Just-in-time meetings: backlog replenishment, continuous improvement meetings, quality circles
2. Asynchronous cadences: daily standups, backlog refinement, retrospectives
3. Cadences synchronized with other teams: daily standups, release demos

Just-in-time meetings are often scheduled on short notice — "hey, let's refine a couple of backlog items after lunch today" — which can be difficult if you are working with multiple teams or multiple clients. Cadenced meetings on the other hand can be scheduled months in advance. For this reason, we have found it best to set up cadenced meetings during the coaching period also when working with Kanban teams.

Each of these touchpoints bring together the whole team or a subset of the team and provide a great opportunity for you to observe or interact with them. Don't give them up too easily! New Scrum teams often think that some of the built-in activities are obsolete or boring and want to skip them. If that happens, we suggest that you ground the discussion with the team in the values and principles in the Agile Manifesto ("Agile Manifesto," 2001). Together, figure out which values and which principles are behind each of the activities they want to skip. If the proposed change does not undermine those values and principles, just go for it. Otherwise a better option would be to figure out new and better ways to meet the values and principles.

When observing your team, it's useful to look at team dynamics, what they talk about and the energy levels. We often use the following "cheat sheet" of questions, adapted from Lyssa Adkins (2010):

- Is everyone who wants to getting the time to speak? Are there dominant people in the room who need to listen more? Are there quiet voices that want to be heard?
- Are the ideas of high quality or are people simply going with the easiest solution?
- Is the team moving toward the simplest solution possible? Or are they going future-proof and gold plating it too?
- Is the team getting tired? Do they need a break?
- Is the atmosphere getting tense? Do they need some comic relief?
- Is the team being audacious enough? Do they come up with great ideas or break through barriers? Or are they avoiding taking a risk?
- Are they taking on as much as they could or are they letting "accepted" barriers get in the way?

- Is the team considering things in terms of customer value? Or in terms of their own effort?
- Are they stuck? Do they need a new perspective, one that brings them more possibilities?

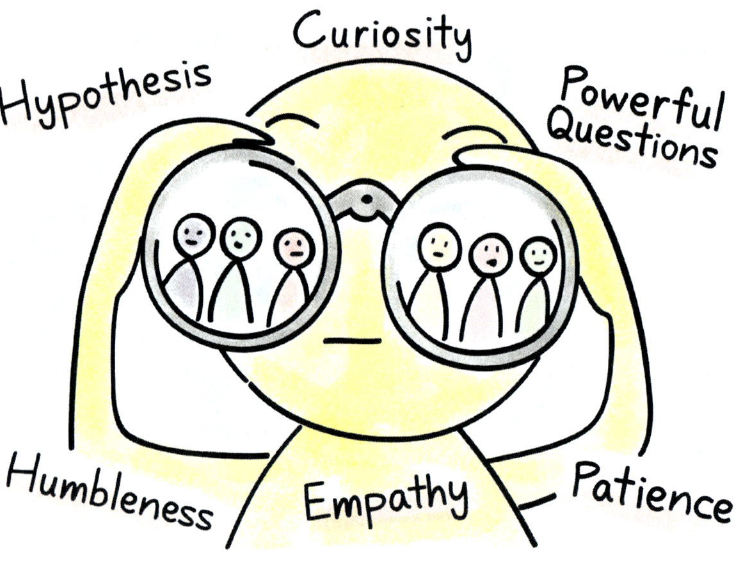

Figure 6.2: Making observations

This is intended to be a starter kit of observation points. Keep this list of observation questions handy, somewhere that you can quickly access it when a conversation just happens around you. Over time, you will come up with your own observation questions arising from what you observe. For example, if you work with several teams in the same company, you may notice that they behave similarly. Add your questions to this list and share them with fellow agile coaches.

6.2 Daily standup

The daily standup is a short-term planning meeting. Although the meeting is not exclusive to agile methods, it's an integral part of many agile methods including Scrum, Kanban and XP.

For an agile coach, the daily meeting forms a great opportunity to observe the team and ask some coaching questions. Let the meeting run its course while you observe and listen, make notes and form hypotheses. While every team is different, there are some items to keep in mind:

- Situation: Does the team report to itself or the ScrumMaster? Is the situation presented honestly? Do they have facts and information in front of them? Is the granularity right (tasks less than one day in length)?
- Focus: Is the goal clear? Is the team focusing on getting the next backlog item done, rather than ensuring everyone has work for the day? Is there a lot of bureaucratic overhead?
- Speaking: Does everyone get the opportunity to speak? Who speaks most, who is most silent? Do people listen intently or are they just waiting for their own turn? Are people supporting each other?
- Decision-making: Who makes decisions? Is it one person or the whole team? Do they evaluate multiple options? Are decisions based on facts? If they make assumptions, do they go on to validate the decisions before investing time?
- Language: Does the team have their own "slang"? Does the body language support the verbal message?
- Trust: Are they showing respect for each other and for other teams? Are they having fun together? Are they able to bring up difficult topics? Are they showing courage?

Standups are also a good moment to evaluate team agreements, for example retrospective action points, daily goals, checking burndown charts, urgent tickets or any other things the team agreed to check daily.

If you have something to discuss with the team or just want to share your observations, you can ask them to stay on for a few more minutes after the meeting. It's polite to make this request before the meeting starts.

Try this

- Focus on the work, not the worker. Avoid asking each person on the team to give a status report; focus instead on the stories and priorities.
- Pass a ball (or some token) around to indicate whose turn it is to speak and to add dynamics to the daily standup.
- Team members should be speaking and making eye contact with each other, not reporting to the ScrumMaster.
- If the team is not finding the meeting useful, find the root cause and fix it, rather than abandoning the meeting. Often the granularity of the tasks does not match the frequency of the meeting or people do not see the need to collaborate.
- Use a "parking lot" for discussions that are too long or do not concern the whole team. Keep the stand-up focused, finish it on time and then anyone who needs to continue the parked discussions can do so after the meeting is over. Anyone has the right to call "time out".
- Towards the end of the meeting, ask questions like: "Which story are you going to finish next?" or "Do you have in front of you all the information you need to make good decisions?"

6.3 Refinement and planning

The Sprint planning and backlog refinement meetings are strongly focused on product questions. Your role as an agile coach is initially to facilitate the meeting, helping the team and stakeholders have productive discussions and make good decisions about the product.

At the same time, you will show the ScrumMaster how to run a good planning meeting. Over time, as the team learns what the planning meeting is about, coaching the ScrumMaster will become your primary focus point. Eventually you can step back and let the ScrumMaster take the lead.

We would like to point out that an agile coach should not get involved in product design questions. The problems inherent in advising and consulting were discussed in sec. 2.2. You should help the team learn the tools and methods they need (coaching and training) and help them bring out information if necessary (facilitating). You can also provide options if you receive a direct question, but it's not your job to design the product.

6.4 Retrospectives

As we mentioned in the introductory chapter, this book is mostly about coaching and not so much about the agile practices. However, good retrospectives are so important that we have decided to make an exception that proves the rule.

During a retrospective teams inspect and adapt both their methods and the way they work together as a team. In an iterative development approach like Scrum, a team runs retrospectives at the end of each iteration. In a flow based approach like Kanban, the cadence for feedback meetings is defined by the policies agreed on by the team(s), like, for instance, a bi-weekly Service Delivery Review.

The primary reason for digging deeper into the topic of retrospectives here is simply that they are a key characteristic of agile teams. An ineffective team that continuously improves will, in the end, beat an effective team that doesn't. All truly agile organizations that we are aware of take their retrospectives very seriously — sometimes almost to the point of becoming religious about them. If you do only one thing as an agile coach, make sure it's getting the team to run effective retrospectives and take responsibility for their own ways of working.

Secondly, retrospectives are key engagement point for agile coaches and a great opportunity to use structured coaching conversations as discussed in sec. 3.5, sec. 3.6 and sec. 4.2. Thirdly, retrospectives are one of the simpler ways of achieving continuous process improvement (CPI). This in turn is explicitly mentioned in Agile Principle #12: "At regular intervals, the team reflects on how to become more effective, then tunes and adjusts its behavior accordingly."

Safety first

Retrospectives are typically facilitated by a ScrumMaster or an agile coach. The facilitator needs to establish a safe environment where trust, transparency and openness allows each person to contribute equally. While always remaining neutral in discussions, the facilitator observes the room and the dynamics of the group, helping them reach the goal.

It is important to understand that the retrospective is about learning and looking ahead, not about blaming and looking back. Norman Kerth has captured this intention perfectly in the *the prime directive of retrospectives*:

> **"We understand and truly believe that everyone did the best job they could, given what they knew at the time, their skills and abilities, the resources available, and the situation at hand."**
> **– Norman Kerth**

This quote emphasizes the fact that people learn through trial and error. There are complex situations that cannot be solved in any other way than by actions or experiments. The outcome might be obvious in hindsight, where we always have 20/20 vision, but the prime directive helps us remember that it wasn't so simple at the time. The quote continues:

"At the end of a project everyone knows so much more. Naturally we will discover decisions and actions we wish we could do over. This is wisdom to be celebrated, not judgement used to embarrass."
— Norman Kerth

We often start retrospectives by reminding the participants of the prime directive.

Retrospective Formats

The format and structure of each retrospective may be different and each team will typically have its own way of doing it. The key goal is to make the meeting a team learning event, fostering change through concrete actions.

One way to keep the retrospectives interesting is to have several different kinds of retros: quick, standard and deep. *Quick retrospectives* are done ad hoc, in 5-10 minutes. The goal is to understand what is happening and find a quick win. You can use powerful questions (see sec. 3.6) to guide the discussion or the Cynefin model, Delta-Plus or Five Whys[1] to generate insights that you can later delve deeper into.

[1] http://en.wikipedia.org/wiki/5_Whys

For *standard retrospectives* on a weekly or biweekly basis, you might use the Starfish or Speedboat models[2] to create suggestions, then dot vote and form the top suggestion(s) into experiments, pilots or SMART Actions. As an alternative you could facilitate an open discussion using either the 5D model (as explained in sec. 4.2), or the Karl Tomm model (sec. 3.6), again making sure that you end up with actionable items.

It's important to run *deep retrospectives* every now and then. They are often run by the book — "Agile Retrospectives" by Derby and Larsen (2006) — and can take several hours. The Derby & Larsen model includes five stages, which we will describe below. If the group is small enough to hold a single coherent discussion, the 5D and Karl Tomm models can again be very useful. In larger retrospectives, it is important to *think global and act local.* In practice there is often a preparatory meeting or team survey for collecting data. After that the data is collated centrally and some basic analysis is carried out. The teams reconvene the following day to generate insights and plan actions.

The five stages of a Retrospective

1. Set the stage

The aim here is to welcome people, make them feel comfortable, break the ice and create a good, safe environment to get everyone involved in the retrospective. It also helps to trigger people to start thinking about the past sprint in a light way.

Some examples:

- We can remind ourselves of our team values
- Remind everyone about the prime directive

[2] Look up Starfish or Speedboat on http://www.plans-for-retrospectives.com/.

- Ask powerful questions, e.g. if you had to represent the sprint as a weather report, what would it be?

2. Gather data

Once we have people engaged, it's time to take a step deeper into the details. You want to elicit as much information from the group as possible. The facilitator can also bring data to the table for the team to discuss.

Examples:

- Look at some metrics, for example velocity, throughput, lead time or quality
- Review the actions from the last retrospective
- 4L's: what I Liked, Learned, Lacked, and Longed for

3. Generate insights

In this phase it about making sense of the collected details. We try to distinguish symptoms from root causes and to discover patterns.

Possible approaches:

- 3H's: what Helped, what Hindered, and what Hypotheses do we have for improving?
- Timeline: plot the collected data on a timeline and identify patterns
- Starfish: what should we Start, Stop, Continue, do More, do Less of?

4. Decide what to do

Once we have figured out what the problems are we need to find out what to do about them so that we can prevent this from happening again.

- Prioritize! Write SMART actions
- Goal - Action: Define a long term goal plus a concrete action for next sprint
- Update agreements: Working Agreements, Definition of Done, etc.

5. Closing

Since we may have had some heated discussions or shared some sensitive personal details, we want to formally "close the box". For the facilitator, it might also be good to ask for feedback from the team and thank people for participating.

- Appreciations: ask people to share something they appreciate about another team member.
- One word: state one word about the Sprint or the Retrospective.
- Return On Time Invested (ROTI): Ask people how much they learned and improved in this retrospective.

Summary

In retrospectives, participants look at the process and discuss what worked and what did not, trying to understand the reasons for each. They then make hypotheses about how to address problems and define actions that could solve them. To make this happen it is crucial to clearly define the goal, who is responsible for achieving it, what is the timeframe and which metrics will be used to verify the outcome. The status of these action items should be checked at each following retrospective.

It is important, from time to time, to leave room for new independent, innovative ideas and experiments to improve the process.

Chapter 7

Structured coaching

Some agile coaches have a fantastic memory. They remember exactly where they left off and are able to pick up the trail where they left off. Not all of us have this gift. In fact, we think that this gift is becoming exceedingly rare. As you work on and off with lots of different teams, it is very easy to lose your way or forget important details. Everyone, including the memory geniuses and the multitaskers, can benefit from some structure in their work.

The "Team Coaching Framework" (TCF) is our way of introducing that structure to the work we do. For individual coaches, the coaching structure serves as a memory aid in intermittent engagements. In pairs or small groups of coaches, the coaching structure forms a basis for collaboration. ScrumMasters, line managers and coaches can pool their observations, draw up hypotheses together, agree on the tools to be used and then carry out actions designed to gently nudge the team towards the same goal.

The structure also allows sharing experiences and ideas for improvement with members of an organization or the larger professional community. In effect, you can take an anonymous coaching structure and discuss the content with any other ScrumMaster or agile coach, regardless of whether they are involved with the same client or not. This allows two or more coaches to learn from each other and enables more experienced coaches to mentor a less experienced coach.

TCF is based on the Observe, Orient, Decide, Act (OODA) loop[1] because it allows us to commit late. There are also goal-oriented methods that follow the better known Plan, Do, Check, Act (PDCA)

[1] http://en.wikipedia.org/wiki/OODA_loop

cycle, but the PDCA cycle forces early commitment — we need to plan up front, before we have enough facts. In the OODA loop we can continuously add more observations as we go and change our hypotheses and goals as necessary.

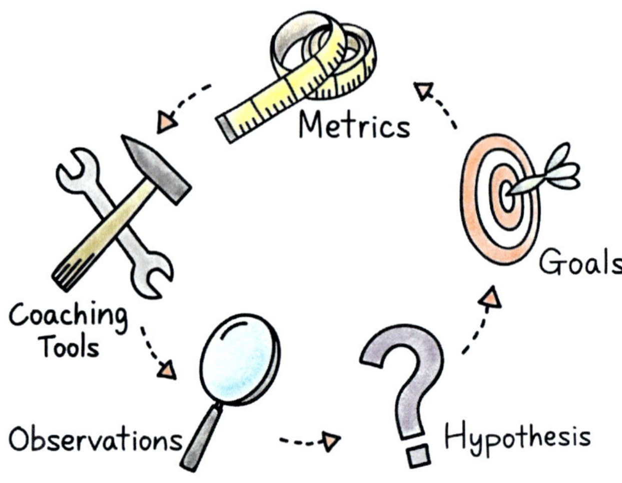

Figure 7.1: The OODA loop when coaching a team

This approach works especially well in complex environments. New agile teams tend to need help with their dysfunctions first. Only after they have started working well enough together as a Scrum team does it make sense to draw up goals and start working together towards them.

Note that there can be many different ways of introducing structure. TCF is something that we have constructed over many years of successes and failures. It's not perfect, but it serves us well. Doubtless it will keep evolving in the future.

7.1 Overview

TCF relies on **Coaching Tools**. These are methods, techniques, workshop formats, etc. that an agile coach can introduce to change the behavior of a team. You can find a collection of coaching tools in the *agile42 TCF Tool* that we have developed[2].

The question arises when to use a specific tool, or, from another perspective, what tool to use in this specific context and situation? TCF uses **Coaching Cards** to bind together a context and a couple of coaching tools. The coaching card template, shown in fig. 7.2, is very simple. It merely consists of four fields or headings. We sometimes use an A4 card for this, sometimes a brief text document. Several coaching cards make up a **Coaching Structure**. The coaching structure can also contain an introduction in the form of a description of the context and the background situation.

We usually create new coaching cards when coaching teams, but since there are situations that recur every so often, we have found it helpful to create a small library of such cards that we can reuse.

The process of creating a coaching card or a coaching structure goes generally from observations through hypotheses and goals to metrics and finally, actions and coaching tools. Be prepared to jump back and forth though, as you may unearth new information or come up with new hypotheses. Next up, we will describe the general steps of creating a coaching card and thereby a coaching structure.

7.2 Make observations

A good coach always starts by observing the team or individual you are coaching. Don't be afraid to collaborate with others on collecting and sharing observations. Multiple people can throw in their

[2] https://tcf.agile42.com/

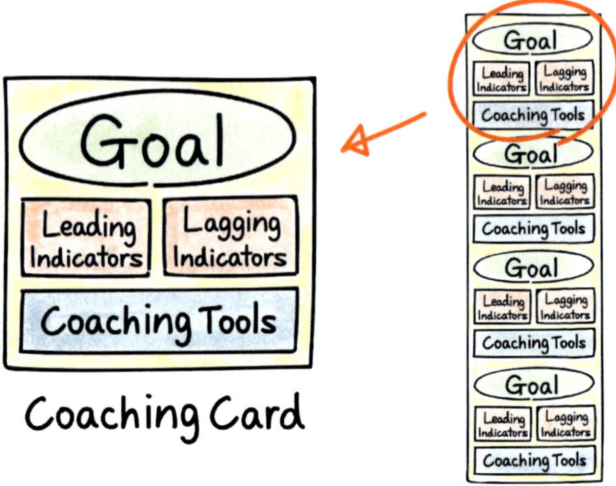

Figure 7.2: Coaching structure

observations and, in doing so, build a better basis for the coaching structure.

An observation is some information that you have seen, remembered or recorded, or received from a data system or from another person. Observations are facts: things either happened or they did not happen. As such they are beyond dispute. People may have different observations and different understandings of why things happened in certain ways, but we will discuss that in the next section.

What to observe? Anything that seems significant to you, including the elephant in the corner of the room. This would include:

- Team interactions — who is talking, who is not?
- Voice and intonation
- Postures and energy levels
- What do people talk about? What do they leave unsaid?

- What information do people look at? What do they ignore?
- Significant events originating inside or outside the team
- Who makes decisions? Is the team deferring to others? How are decisions communicated?

When to observe? The best time is any time and all the time! In sec. 6, we mentioned that different frameworks (Scrum, Kanban etc.) can give you several different touchpoints with the team. Use all the opportunities you get. Don't forget to talk with stakeholders, specialists and neighbouring teams.

How to collect information and observations is up to you. Many of us write diaries or record our engagements and interactions some other way. We use pen and paper, post-its, tablets, cellphone cameras, pocket/system cameras, e-mail, etc. to collect data. Then we aggregate the information into a reliable and secure collaboration environment to share with colleagues and/or clients.

When observing, you should be aware of something called *observation bias*, which means that the observer allows her own ideas to influence what she observes or how she interprets the observations. In practice, it means that people are more eager to take in facts that support their own points of view. If you like knitting, you would subscribe to knitting magazines, blogs and podcasts, and perhaps avoid those about car tuning or technical physics.[3]

There are some tricks you can use to avoid observation bias. Try this:

- Avoid drawing any conclusions until you have a good amount of observations
- Entertain multiple hypotheses and be prepared to change them

[3] If you are a technical physicist who likes knitting and car tuning, let us know and we will change this example.

- Share and compare observations and conclusions with other coaches
- Validate each and every hypothesis before you expend significant energy on them

7.3 Formulate a hypothesis

Now that you have some observations, you can start thinking about what would explain the observed behaviors. Draw up an explanation that is coherent and follows the observations. This is not always straightforward and can require a lot of thinking, and support from others. Many of the retrospective "Gather insights" methods work well here, for example Five Whys, Fishbone or Force Field Analysis.

Always try to validate or invalidate your hypotheses before you commit to it and start constructing a goal. Search for for additional information that can strengthen or weaken it. The OODA loop allows you to dig up more data and reformulate your hypotheses as needed. Make more observations and talk to people to get more information. The flip side is that you shouldn't get too attached to your hypotheses. Always be prepared to throw them away and start from scratch.

Share observations and collaborate with other people as they can help you come up with a wider range of hypotheses or help (in)validate a hypothesis you have made. If you have access to a co-coach or mentor, you can learn a lot by discussing your observations and hypotheses with them. Again, remember that while facts are facts, different people may have different interpretations and opinions of those facts.

Over time, you will learn to see patterns that are recurring within the organization or across organizations. Experienced agile coaches have seen many different situations and have learned what is likely to help in each situation.

If you end up with several coherent hypotheses, you may want to create a separate coaching card for each hypothesis and construct a coaching structure from the cards. If they are aligned, you can just merge them into the same document and call it your coaching structure.

7.4 Identify a goal

From the hypothesis, it is usually quite easy to construct a goal. Given the context and the hypothesis, what is the behavior we want to see in the team? Try to phrase this as a transforming question or statement, rather than a problem-solving one. (Please see sec. 4.2 for a description of transforming questions.)

The goal can be lofty but should not be too abstract — rather than "world peace and happiness," you may want to aim for "ceasefire agreement." The reason for loftiness is that you may not actually reach the goal before the coaching structure becomes irrelevant. As the team improves along the chosen dimension, the Theory of Constraints by Goldratt and Cox (2004) says that another dysfunction will eventually pop up and become the most important bottleneck, which means that you will need to create new coaching cards and structures as you go. For the same reason, you should avoid making KPIs or incentives out of these goals. The reason for having pragmatic goals is that abstract goals can be very difficult to work towards — you may have to work along several dimensions to get there and getting there can take too much time.

7.5 Define metrics

Metrics are integral to the idea of coaching cards and coaching structures. We define the metrics immediately after we have agreed on a goal, not after defining the actions, otherwise we run the risk of choosing metrics that measure the actions we take, rather than the goals we want to reach. We recommend that you use at least one lagging indicator and a handful of leading indicators. And what are leading and lagging indicators? Let's approach this topic through an example.

The problem with most metrics is that they can be measured only *after* we have an outcome and this may be too late. For example, many organizations measure the quality level of their software by making a release candidate, then having a cadre of testers run regression tests. Because manual testing is expensive, releases are done as seldom as possible and the longer they go between releases, the longer the bugs go undetected.

The number of found and unfixed bugs in the software is a very common **lagging indicator**. But by the time you get around to counting the bugs, it is too late — the bugs are already in the software. You need to root them out one by one and then test again to ensure they are gone and to hunt for additional bugs hiding behind the first ones.

As you can imagine, it would be very useful to get some early indications of what the quality level is likely to be. What should we look for? Here are some ideas:

- The number of automated tests — two tests are more likely to find a bug than one test
- Code coverage for automated tests — better code coverage means that more bugs are likely to be found and fixed within the Sprints, rather than in system testing
- Cyclomatic complexity — low CC indicates simpler code that is easier to understand and, thereby, is less likely to have bugs
- Bug fixing rate — the more bugs we fix and the faster we fix them, the fewer bugs we are likely to have in the product

These are what we call **leading indicators**. They are indirect measurements of things that are associated with or correlated to what we want to achieve. Leading indicators are also *probabilistic* — there is a chance that each individual indicator is wrong, so we need to look at them in aggregate. For example, even if the bug fixing rate looks good, the bug introduction rate could be even higher.

We do not need to figure out the exact probabilities however. For our purposes it is enough to use many different leading indicators and check what they show as an aggregate. Leading indicators can sometimes also help us understand alternative ways of achieving our goal.

You will find it comparatively easy to come up with lagging indicators for the coaching card or coaching structure. However, leading indicators often leave people stumped. To make matters worse, you need at least three and preferably five or more of them. We would advise you to look at what people do, what they discuss and the words they choose. We sometimes use the "miracle question" to find ideas: assuming that the problem was fixed overnight, how would you notice that things were going the right way?

It is important to make all metrics very clear and actionable. Saying "progress is updated regularly" is a good start, but not in itself sufficient. Instead you could say "in the daily standup, the ScrumMaster notes whether the Sprint board was up to date or not when the standup started."

7.6 Choose the coaching tools

As mentioned in the overview, tools are methods, techniques, workshop formats etc. that you can introduce to permanently change the behavior of a team. Because of this very loose definition, the list of potential coaching tools is very long — theoretically infinite.

At agile42, we maintain a repository of 100+ central, well-defined tools[4] that we expect all our coaches to learn and know. Several dozen of these we use weekly if not daily and there are also many unlisted tools that we use occasionally. We also sometimes combine components into ad-hoc, hybrid tools or create new tools on the spur of the moment.

By observing and talking to other coaches, you may learn about new tools that you can try out and make part of your toolbox. Other good sources are blog posts and other books.

7.7 Build a coaching structure

At this stage, you have all the information you need to make a coaching card. Take a piece of paper or a text editor, write down the five headings and fill in the rest. This is straight-forward manual labor that should not pose any challenges. Don't write a novel though, usually one or two paragraphs will be more than sufficient.

If you have more than one coaching card, you can combine them into a coaching structure. It is often sensible to merge the context descriptions into a separate section at the start of the document:

1. Context
2. Coaching card A
    1. Hypothesis
    2. Goal
    3. Metrics
    4. Tools
3. Coaching card B
    1. Hypothesis

[4] https://tcf.agile42.com/

    2. …

4. Coaching card C

    1. …

7.8 Follow up

If your hypothesis is wrong, this will usually become apparent at the latest when you start applying the coaching tools. Be prepared to change or even scrap the whole coaching card and make new observations to refine your hypotheses.

It takes two weeks to build a habit. When the coaching tools are applied consistently and regularly — on a daily or sprintly basis — you should start seeing changes and improvements within the first sprint, and they should be established after a couple of sprints.

You may need to swap out metrics as you go. Don't be afraid of adding or removing leading indicators. Because lagging indicators measure the actual outcome, you may want to stick to them for longer periods of time in order to build up long-term historical data.

As the team grows and the context changes, the coaching card eventually outlives its usefulness. As mentioned previously, the Theory of Constraints by Goldratt and Cox (2004) states that every system has one major bottleneck that constrains the whole system. As you remove or reduce this bottleneck, another takes its place and working further on the original bottleneck will not improve the system. There will come a time when you must archive the current coaching structure and create a new one.

Is it OK to share a coaching structure with the team? It depends. There's nothing that prevents you from sharing the structure, but you might get unanticipated side effects. For example, it might affect the team's behavior adversely or they might start gaming the metrics. On the upside, they could also take the desired change to heart and make it part of their team goal. In general, however, we would advise keeping the coaching structure as a tool for the eyes of the ScrumMaster and related stakeholders only. This is because the team already has a mechanism for improvement (the retrospective meeting) but the ScrumMaster doesn't really have anything.

If you really want to take something up with the team, you can kick off a retrospective by telling them what you have observed. This is usually a safe approach that is appreciated by the team. Before you start, remember to ask if they want your feedback, and respect their decision. Also make sure that they understand that you are merely stating your observations and not making any judgements. We find that most teams appreciate the information, and are able to hold good and constructive conversations about it.

7.9 Case studies for TCF

In this section, we will present a number of case studies from which you might be inspired. Each of the case studies is described just as we would prepare a coaching card. This includes the observation (context), the hypothesis, the goal, the metrics and the tools involved.

Coaching card: The hurried tests

Context:

At the review meeting the team demonstrates a product that has not been fully tested. The tests are never ready. Often the tests are run on the tester's machine or on the developer's laptop. They never describe the test environment nor do they reflect the normal production situation. There is no report on the tests run to verify the product. The Product Owner seems to be okay with this and the ScrumMaster says that the time is so short that "it is a miracle that they have time to test anything".

Hypothesis:

We think the team does not fully understand the principles behind the XP practices. Also it seems that there is considerable technical debt, which is preventing the team from investing enough time in test automation and checking the quality of the delivered User Stores. We believe the lack of automated tests results in a fear of making mistakes.

Goal:

The Scrum Team is delivering with higher quality and faster than before. Thanks to a Continuous Integration infrastructure, they have developed a sense of safety which improves their focus on value and performance in implementing new features. Automation is perceived as having a great value by all the teams working on the software platform, even those that are not yet using agile methods. The number of defects after deployment have decreased dramatically and teams have more time to deliver value.

Metrics:

Leading indicators:

- The Development Team operates a continuous integration (CI) server on which the latest software is automatically deployed and uses this for the Sprint Review demonstrations.
- There are automated build and test scripts within the CI server. The team receives feedback on the quality of the code within minutes of check-in.
- For every User Story, the Development Team creates at least one automated functional test.
- For every change in the code, the Development Team creates several new unit tests.

Lagging indicators:

- The Development Team is delivering consistently with higher quality.
- The number of interruptions during the Sprint due to defects and problems in production has decreased significantly if not disappeared completely.
- The code coverage level is high and increasing.
- The team is of the opinion that the Continuous Integration infrastructure helps them develop faster and with higher quality.

Coaching Tools:

- TDD Workshop: Introduce TDD practices in a safe-to-fail environment, so that the team not only understands the principles, but can also apply them.
- Slow Lane: Pick one lower priority User Story for which the team commits to "dot the I's and cross the T's"… which includes writing proper automated tests.
- Reproduce bugs: The team agrees to write tests first to reproduce the most severe defects, and then fix the defects so that they can immediately prove that the fix works. The tests are added to the test suite in order to prevent regression.

Coaching card: Team reports to ScrumMaster

Context:

Team members report to the ScrumMaster in the daily standup. Excepting one or two senior engineers, the others do not ask or volunteer information. The ScrumMaster takes a very controlling role in the meeting, walking everyone through the three questions.

When needed, he tells the team what the managers are saying, doing and thinking about some issues ("Manager N.N. called the customer yesterday and they will decide... so don't do anything before you get an e-mail."). He is quick to delegate work and ends the meeting by asking if everyone has "enough work for today". The ScrumMaster is a former Project Manager and took his CSM around 8 months ago.

Hypotheses:

1) We think that the ScrumMaster has not internalized the mechanisms that he is expected to use. He may have difficulties understanding the role and the dynamics between ScrumMaster and Dev Team.

2) The ScrumMaster is used to being the hub of information between "managers" and "coders" and is afraid of losing that position.

3) The team may be afraid of taking responsibility, and is happy to hand it to the ScrumMaster.

4) There are indications that the managers see the dev teams as a cost sink rather than a value source. That is, the managers are more concerned about how the coders spend their time rather than what they produce.

Goal:

The goal is to make the team members talk to each other rather than the ScrumMaster and to plan their Sprints and workdays as a team.

Metrics:

Leading indicators:

- What percentage of questions in the standup are posed by the ScrumMaster compared to team members?
- How often do the team members say “us” and “we” rather than “me” and “I”?
- How often does the ScrumMaster NOT ask if everyone has work for the day?
- Ask the ScrumMaster to skip a daily standup. Silently observe the meeting when the ScrumMaster is not present. Do the interactions change?

Lagging indicators:

- All work items are pulled by team members, not pushed by the ScrumMaster
- The ScrumMaster listens more than he speaks
- Managers interact with the team directly, not through the ScrumMaster

Coaching Tools:

- Teach the ScrumMaster in the role.
- Role-model for the ScrumMaster. Offer to run the daily standups a couple of times, then explain to him what you did and why.
- Gently move the ScrumMaster outside the circle in the daily standup. If team members still turn towards the ScrumMaster, move him all the way behind the speaking team member.
- Talk to the ScrumMaster to find out what stakeholders he is reporting to. Then systematically meet all stakeholders and work with them to replace the reports with transparency.
- Help the team create a pull policy.
- In a safe setting, discuss with the ScrumMaster how he feels about the changed responsibilities, then help the ScrumMaster choose the right path forward.

- Educate managers on value-focus vs. cost-focus and the implications of each.

Coaching card: Weak collaboration in the team

Context:

The team opens up multiple Sprint Backlog items in parallel and have problems finishing them by the end of the Sprint. There is no collective feeling of responsibility and people hold back on asking for help because the other team members are all busy with their own tasks and would not have time to help anyway.

This attitude, combined with the size of the stories, generates the behaviour that individuals feel overwhelmed and focus primarily on completing their own tasks. Those few who are done early polish their own work or open new stories before helping others. Most of the time, it is too late to get a story done by the end of the Sprint. Furthermore, as there are no consequences from not delivering a story, the stories get dragged along from Sprint to Sprint.

Hypothesis:

The team is more interested in being efficient as individuals, as opposed to being effective as a team. This leads to many dysfunctions.

The team does not understand the meaning of commitment and does not understand their collective responsibility. Therefore, they fail to manage the risk and to control the process properly.

Goal:

The goal is to learn to appreciate team effectiveness. Helping each other to move collectively forward is the first priority of the team.

Metrics:

Leading indicators

- Team members are actively seeking someone to pair with on tasks (active collaboration), rather than waiting to ask for help until the Sprint is almost over and the PO and stakeholders are starting to ask questions (passive).
- No more than three stories are in progress simultaneously.
- When you enter the room, you will regularly see team members working in pairs or small groups on the same computer.

Lagging indicators

- The hit rate of the Sprint (number of stories delivered vs. planned) stabilizes at 90% or above
- The variance of the velocity goes down. In other words, the velocity curve becomes smoother and exhibits less zig-zagging than it does now.
- The velocity keeps increasing over time. The trend can be slow but is positive.

Coaching Tools:

- Create a Skills Matrix and use it to promote collaboration for improved knowledge transfer
- Use the Working Agreement to limit the number of stories started during a Sprint. In case of exceptions, note them down and discuss them at the Retrospective. This will encourage collaboration on a single story (including testing very early).
- Add pair work on tasks to the Working Agreement for better quality (building quality in).
- Agree that each task or User Story needs to be the responsibility of two people rather than one and make sure this can be visualized on the board.
- Highlight tasks dependencies at the planning meeting (use sequential numbering and flow sequence).

- Write down the Sprint Goal as a marketing motto and hang it in the team room. Challenge the team to pull stories and evaluate multiple options to achieve the Sprint Goal.

Chapter 8

Challenges

As agile coaches, we often face challenges — one could argue that that is what the job is about. But even assuming that you yourself feel comfortable in your role as an agile coach and teacher and have the tools and structures you need to do your job, you will often encounter other people who are wary, scared or doubtful or simply have a different understanding of what has happened and what needs to be done next.

This chapter explores a couple of models that have helped us understand why people react as they do to change and specifically to agile adoptions and transformations. We will also look at some techniques for lowering the resistance to change: constructing change proposals, building consensus, anchoring ideas, running safe-to-fail experiments and getting buy-in.

We will open this chapter by discussing two thinking models that are useful for understanding why people resist change: the Lizard Brain and SCARF.

8.1 The lizard brain

All humans have a hard-wired notion that change is dangerous. Over-reacting pays off in the jungle or on the veldt — those who scram away without thinking have a good chance of seeing their offspring grow up. And so we have evolved a mechanism for getting ourselves out of dangerous situations quickly and with a minimum of thinking. In fact, thinking is high on the list of things *not* to do. Those who start analyzing whether the waving grass really

Figure 8.1: Coaching challenges

does conceal a man-eating saber-tooth tiger are more likely to end up analyzing the tiger from the inside.

Change and fear are connected on quite a deep level in our brains. As shown in fig. 8.2, when subjected to a threat of some kind — a threat to their habits, territory, or very existence — people go into panic mode and will either fight, flee or freeze. Like all models, this model is incomplete: it's a simplification of reality and full of holes and errors. However, we have found it very useful. It explains some of the reasons why people fear change, and also helps make sense of why people react as they do in the face of change.

The name *lizard brain* comes from fact that panic reactions are handled (mostly) by a part of the brain called the *amygdala*, which can be found just above the brainstem in all vertebrates. We share the amygdala with all mammals, birds and — as the name implies — with lizards.

Figure 8.2: The lizard brain — primal reactions

When a vertebrate animal is subjected to a strong threat, the amygdala causes an immediate primal reaction. This is not a simple reflexive action: reflexes typically only yank a couple of muscles. But the primal reaction is still well below rational thought. The amygdala in fact *prevents rational thought* by subverting and disconnecting the upper brain functions. People suffering from primal fear are not only unreceptive to rational arguments but actually incapable of rational thought.

Interestingly enough for an agile coach, similar patterns can be found in prolonged situations of uncertainty, fear or anxiety, as is the case in e.g. agile deployments. Case in point: "We will pilot Scrum in the organization and your team is the best candidate!" In other words: "We say you Scrum." Ouch! How do people interpret this?

Habits — Most people are initially vary of agile methods as they need to change their own working habits. Harsh corporate environments cause people to form their own patterns and strategies for survival and they may be very suspicious of "team work" and "collaboration".

For example, we regularly meet engineers who have learned not to ever give honest estimates. They have formed habits of hiding the actual state of their work, giving vague reports like "90% done but we have some technical problems" or having a perpetual "coding" task that they move back and forth on the task board.[1] Others feel that the daily standups are stupid — it takes weeks to implement this feature anyway so what need is there to report every day?

Territory — Scrum can also be a threat to people's territory. Former project managers that are now relabeled ScrumMasters or Product Owners suddenly find that they have lost a large portion of their former decision power. Deep specialists are forced to open up their work to the scrutiny of others. Software architects find that teams are doing unauthorized changes directly into the code base.

Existence — Some people see agile methods as a threat to their existence in the organization. These include line managers whose teams are suddenly self-organizing; testers who learn that all testing will soon be automated; or specialists who learn that they are in fact not so special.

To the vast majority that is not directly involved in driving the agile transition, Scrum is a cause of anxiety or outright fear. How do they respond?

Fight — Direct and indirect attacks. Badmouthing. Spreading fear, uncertainty and doubt. Passive-aggressive behavior in the

[1] When we see a task named "coding", this gives us the signal that the team is tracking how they spend time rather than the outcome they produce.

Scrum meetings. "Here, let me help you with that... oops, so sorry." Appearing to play along for a while, then a sudden explosion of this-will-never-work. And so on — the examples are countless.

Flee — Some people grab the opportunity and move to other teams or escape the company altogether. The decision to flee is often made early, sometimes as soon as the news has broken, but it can take months for the fallout to appear. By the time people start understanding and accepting the new methods, they have already made new commitments and signed new contracts, and the decision is no longer reversible.

Freeze — A surprisingly large number of people seem to lose their drive and become unable to produce anything of value for months on end. They are tapping on the keyboard and moving the mouse but nothing real comes out.

In almost every team we work with, we find examples of fighting, freezing and sometimes, but luckily very seldom, also of fleeing. This model has helped us make sense of why people behave irrationally during an agile deployment. As an agile coach, it is your job to navigate people past this stage of anxiety. The main problem is how to do that when people are not thinking rationally.

You will need to start by identifying and addressing their concerns, showing that the change is happening on their own terms. We have noticed that it is good to have a brief *meet and greet* with the team before the coaching starts. This could happen in conjunction with some team training or as a stand-alone meeting between 20 and 45 minutes in length. During the meet and greet we go through the upcoming coaching schedule, point out that we are here to support and guide the team, and underline that things will happen on their own terms.

With especially afflicted persons, we have also had good luck with informal one-on-one coffee discussions, alleviating their fears and giving ideas for how to move forward. Sometimes the best approach is to just listen and make it clear that you have heard their concerns. In the end, agile adoption is about teamification and while you may be able to help people find their new positions in the team, there are always going to be people who need to make some hard decisions for themselves.

8.2 SCARF

Because agile methods introduce new patterns of communication and decision power, this will obviously have an impact on the existing social networks and patterns. SCARF is a model for understanding the drivers of human social behavior. In this context it can help explain some of the fears and dislikes people show when subjected to an "agile adoption" or "agile deployment". Although the model itself is well described by David Rock (2008), we will recount the key points here.

Similar to the lizard brain model that we covered previously, SCARF describes low-level threat or reward scenarios in the amygdala: people unconsciously try to minimize threats and maximize rewards. We do this by tagging stimuli as either "good" (associated with rewards) or "bad" (associated with threats) and try to respectively approach or avoid such stimuli. The model, shown in fig. 8.3, contains five different social interaction domains: Status, Certainty, Autonomy, Relatedness and Fairness. We will describe them next.

Status — Your importance relative to other people, pecking order, seniority. High status is linked to lower stress, better health and a longer life. Being subjected to pecking and mobbing

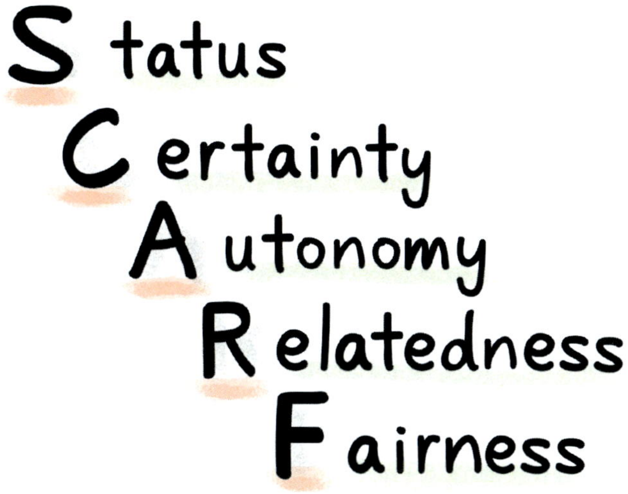

Status
Certainty
Autonomy
Relatedness
Fairness

Figure 8.3: SCARF

activates the same areas as physical pain, and even the perception of a reduction in status can cause a strong threat reaction. People may defend irrational ideas in order to avoid the threat and pain associated with a loss of status.

For example, we often see organizations where projects are strongly linked to the Project Manager or PO, to the point that people talk about “Pete’s project” and “Linda’s project”. Reprioritizing Linda’s project over Pete’s may cause a perceived increase or loss in status, triggering gloating from one and complaints from the other. Fighting to get a position on the most strategically important project becomes more important than collaborating on getting all projects done.

Status is decreased when people receive unwanted instructions or technical advice, or are subjected to public shaming or criticism. Public acknowledgement, recognition, promotions etc. increase status. Working on a well-regarded team can also increase status.

Certainty — Your perceived ability to predict the future. This is important because the brain works as a continuous pattern-matching machine. Your senses continuously give feedback that your brain filters and matches with known patterns, and adjusts your actions accordingly. If something feels out of kilter — e.g. your foot slides sideways when walking — your brain immediately refocuses on the urgent issue. This immediate need takes attention away from your long-term goal. Continuous uncertainty, such as not knowing your role in this new agile process, can disrupt people's ability to produce results.

Because the mere *perception* of predictability is what counts, people are happy to believe in project plans even if they rationally know that the software project failure rate is immense. People are also happy to engage in depth-first problem solving even if width-first problem solving (e.g. the wisdom of crowds) would result in better solutions.

Conflicting visions, overly large goals, time-limited job contracts and organizational changes can increase the uncertainty and make people feel concerned. Clear objectives, reachable goals, credible plans and solid careers increase certainty.

Autonomy — Your sense of being in control of events. This is somewhat similar to Certainty, but reflects your own ability to *control* the future rather than your ability to *predict* it.

Micro-management reduces people's autonomy, which can be very debilitating. Allowing people to arrange their working environment and choose their tools, pick their work tasks, choose their working hours etc. can have a positive effect.

Working in a team also reduces the autonomy because the individuals have less say. However, there are increases in status, certainty, relatedness and fairness that makes the sum total positive.

Relatedness — Your sense of being safe with others, of being surrounded by "friends" rather than "foes". This likely stems from humanoids having lived in tribes and flocks for hundreds of thousands of years, where strangers are potential competitors and likely to cause trouble.

The need for relatedness is a good mechanism for team-building. Having a strong team identity helps, as does informal meetings, water-cooler discussions as well as mentor-style relationships.

In companies with tall hierarchies, long budgeting cycles and complicated incentive systems people can start perceiving other groups as foes. This leads to withholding of information, internal politics and eventually to *siloing*. Specialists who work alone or are often shifted from project to project can also suffer from low relatedness.

Sharing food, alcohol or other mild stimulants help people relate, thereby reducing this threat. For example, in many cultures it is traditional to serve vodka, coffee or tea during important meetings because this helps build a kind of temporary relatedness.

Fairness — Your perception of exchanges being equitable. Unfairness is linked to intense negative emotions such as disgust, which makes this a surprisingly strong dimension of human social interaction. It can drive people to e.g. spend significant spare time on building open-source software, take unpaid leave to volunteer for the Red Cross or throw themselves in front of advancing tanks.

There are many things that can ruin the sense of fairness, including internal politics and unclear strategic decisions. We also see problems related to pay discrepancies, individual incentives and fake rewards i.e. "Employee of the Month" -style awards. For example, a certain company moved their headquarters to the countryside far outside a major metropolitan area. Thousands of employees were forced to take long commutes and were not amused when they noticed that most of the executives lived in an upscale residential area nearby.

Fairness can be increased by improving transparency and communication, by establishing clear expectations, and by having the same rules apply to everyone including top managers.

In an agile transition, the SCARF model can help us understand why different people react in different ways. Traditional command and control organizations are often "business monarchies" or "technical monarchies" which means that managers or technical leads are accustomed to receive the rewards: they enjoy higher status, they provide directions and action plans, they decide who does what, they control the budget, they decide who is in the team and who is not and they can choose to share or withhold information.

The team, on the other hand, is under threat. Their status comes from how well they can serve the manager and they depend on the manager to provide plans for the future. They have little autonomy, receiving designs and action requests from elsewhere. Furthermore, they are often working on individual goals, and things like stack ranking and large discrepancies in pay undermine their sense of relatedness and fairness.

In an agile organization, the most important thing is to ensure that the team can work as effectively as possible. The team receives the rewards, and the managers are there to facilitate and support. This change is both rapid and disruptive, and it may come as a shock to many managers and technical leaders. Often, they try to retain their rewards and avoid the threats by making agile go away.

8.3 Influencing behavior

We have found the two models mentioned above very useful in understanding why people resent the new and scary agile methods. Often the best approach is to sit down over lunch or a cup of coffee and make it clear that while roles are going to change, nobody is getting fired. The people involved will also be in control of the process (after an initial boot-strapping period) and you will be there to help people become proficient.

As an aside, it can help to take a so-called "*yes, and*" approach and build on top of suggestions posed by the organization. Using Microsoft Project for backlog management? Yes — and let's see if it has a team board view. Full traceability from requirements to test cases? Yes — and this means that we should ensure that the requirements are testable (training, workshops, hands-on coaching) and that the traceability report can be generated automatically.

The second half of this chapter covers a couple of more structured approaches. The first approach is to collect data. If the data supports your hypothesis, you have a case for pushing a potential solution. Otherwise, drop it and do something else. The second approach is to design and carry out safe-to-fail experiments, in a way that is transparent and involves as many people as possible in the process. This lowers the friction and resistance.

8.4 Building your case on metrics

> **"All opinions are not equal. Some are a very great deal more robust, sophisticated and well supported in logic and argument than others."**
> **– Douglas Adams**

Many problems are complex, and the more people they involve, the more complex they tend to be. Formally, a complex problem has causal chains that are partially obscured, multi-linked or cyclical. More pragmatically, a complex situation can have several likely causes and the solutions may have unintended side-effects. In a complex situation people can argue for a very long time about the nature of the problem. People may even disagree about whether the problem actually exists or not.

The great quote by Douglas Adams that we chose to open this chapter with states that opinions should be founded in logic and argument. We would like to add to the list and underline the importance of *metrics*. Metrics are the foundation of empirical process control. While opinions can be hashed and rehashed until the cows come home, it is difficult to argue against hard data.

One approach for resolving complex situations is to collect data and quantify the problems. Make a tick on a piece of paper every time something occurs or count the bright red post-its on the board at the end of the sprint. After you have collected enough data, analyze it to see whether the issue is large enough to make into a business case. How many times does this happen per sprint? How much time do we lose and how much does that cost us? How long does it take for our proposed solution to pay itself back?

All things can't be expressed as money, though. One team member was complaining about people entering the big open office area and asking him for directions to other teams and individuals in the area. We asked this team member to note on a piece of paper whenever he felt disturbed. At the end of the sprint, he had to his own surprise barely collected three such incidents. This put the problem into perspective, and he agreed that the issue was smaller than he thought. Even so, the team ideated and executed a couple of solutions, including pasting an area map and a "do not disturb" sign on the wall beside his desk.

8.5 Safe-to-fail experiments

There are several different mechanisms you can rely on in order to lower the threshold and reduce the risk for trying out new things. One such mechanism is to create change proposals collaboratively, so that you get more ideas for proposals and the chosen proposal gets a wide buy-in. We touched on this approach in the chapter on "Structured Coaching" (sec. 7) and it is applicable to all kinds of proposals.

Another mechanism is the approach known as "Which Arm?" The name comes from the question you are asked when donating blood: which arm should we draw the blood from? The end result will be the same in any case — you will lose half a liter of blood — but it gives you the perception of being in control.

How does "Which Arm?" relate to experiments? Well, many companies have a static perspective on organization. They believe that the current setup is stable and that any change requires energy. The more agile approach is to assume that change is inevitable: the question is in which direction to guide it. In the context of organizational change, avoid asking "Shall we try this particular proposal?" and instead try asking "Which of these proposals are we going to try next?" This obviously requires more than one proposal and a method for comparing them.

A third mechanism is to frame the proposal as limited time pilot or experiment. We try it out for a sprint or two and assess whether it is heading towards success or failure. If it looks like it's going to fail, we cut it short and revert to our previous process. If it looks like it's succeeding, we let it run until we are sure, then embed the new method into our ways of working.

It turns out that for a proposal to be a *safe-to-fail experiment* it is essential to have a way of dampening the side effects, a kind of rollback plan. The rollback can be time consuming and expensive but it must be doable. You will also need to list some early indicators of impending failure.

For many years now, we have used the *Cynefin complexity model* for sensemaking by Snowden and Boone (2007). The model has many implications, for example, that organizations are complex and that planning and executing a change program is futile. Organizational change can however be directed. Dave Snowden has created a compact template for defining safe-to-fail experiments aligned with the Cynefin model. It helps ensure that the proposals are coherent and motivated but also that you are watching for early signs of failure and have a solid, clear roll-back plan.

Snowden advocates running several experiments in parallel with different parameters and ensuring that at least one is *oblique* and another is *naïve*. An oblique experiment does not attack the root cause but rather focuses on one or more of the symptoms. This can lead to valuable learning and can be a good approach for problems that look intractable. Naïve experiments are set up without much analysis or even thought. Usually this would involve throwing money (or consultants... but we are repeating ourselves!) at the problem to make it go away.

Have you considered hiring a hex doctor to exorcise the bugs from your code lately? No? It may be a stupid idea, but it is also a valid experiment that is both oblique and naïve. There is no logical analysis behind it and it focuses directly on the issue (bugs) rather than underlying root causes (you are not preventing bugs effectively enough). Experience tells us that this particular experiment is unlikely to work as planned... but in some organizations it could be a useful learning experience with beneficial side effects.

Using all three mechanisms mentioned above, and working on a Kanban board, it is possible to evolve an organization by probing, sensing and adapting.

8.6 Try this

1) At the end of sec. 8.2 we described a traditional command-and-control organization using the SCARF model. What would an agile organization look like? Take a moment with a like-minded colleague/friend and try to build a SCARF case for a hypothetical hyper-agile organization. Then compare the two SCARF cases. What do you see? What could you do to alleviate the issues?

2) Take a moment to refresh your memory on the concepts of coaching cards and coaching structures in sec. 7. How do they differ from the safe-to-fail experiments outlined in this chapter?

References

"So long, and thanks for all the fish."
– The Dolphins in The Hitchhiker's Guide to the Galaxy (and the agile42 coaches)

Adkins, L., 2010. Coaching agile teams: A companion for scrum masters, agile coaches and project managers in transition. Addison-Wesley.

Agile Manifesto, 2001.

Cooperrider, D.L., Whitney, D., 2005. Appreciative inquiry - a positive revolution in change. Berrett-Koehler Publishers.

Derby, E., Larsen, D., 2006. Agile retrospectives: Making good teams great. The Pragmatic Programmers.

Goldratt, E.M., Cox, J., 2004. The goal: A process of ongoing improvement, 20th anniversary. ed. North River Press.

Katzenbach, J., Smith, D., 1993. The wisdom of teams. Harvard Business Review Press.

Kimsey-House, H., Kimsey-House, K., Sandahl, P., Whitworth, L., 2011. Co-active coaching. Nicholas Brealey Publishing.

Ringelmann, M., 1913. Recherches sur les moteurs animés: Travail de l'homme. Annales de l'Institut National Agronomique, 2me série 12, 1–40.

Rock, D., 2008. SCARF: A brain-based model for collaborating with and influencing others. NeuroLeadership Journal 1, 44–52.

Satir, V., 1964. Conjoint family therapy. Science; Behavior Books, Palo Alto, CA.

Sheridan, R., 2013. Joy, inc.: how we built a workplace people love. Penguin.

Snowden, D.J., Boone, M.E., 2007. A leader's framework for decision making. Harvard Business Review.

Stelter, R., Hansen, S.E., Møller, L., Holmgren, A., Rosenkvist, G., Hansen-Skovmoes, P., 2005. Coaching - læring og udvikling. Dansk Psykologisk Forlag.

Storch, J., Søholm, T.M., Juhl, A., Dahl, K., Molly, A., 2006. Ledelsesbaseret coaching. Børsens Forlag.

Tuckman, B.W., 1965. Developmental sequence in small groups. Psychological Bulletin 63, 384–399.

Weick, K.E., Roberts, K.H., 1993. Collective mind in organizations: Heedful interrelating on flight decks. Administrative Science Quarterly 38, 357–381.

West, M.A., 2012. Effective teamwork: Practical lessons from organizational research. John Wiley & Sons.

Made in the USA
Monee, IL
16 July 2021